Coalition Politics in India

First Decade of 21st Century

C. P. Bhambri

SHIPRA

First Published in India in 2010

Rs. 995 ; US$ 39.75

ISBN : 978-81-7541-539-3

2017 Impression

Coalition Politics in India: First Decade of 21st Century

Published by:
SHIPRA PUBLICATIONS
LG 18-19, Pankaj Central Market
I.P. Ext., Patparganj, Delhi 110092, India
Tel.: +91 11 2223 5152/6152
E-mail: info@shiprapublication.com
www.shiprapublication.com

Preface

The main purpose of this study is to demystify the reality of coalition system of government at the Centre and the role of regional parties which are participants in governance at the Centre. Every political party, all-India and regional, is or fractions a representative of various strata of the ruling and exploiting classes and this is the reason that every all-India party like the Congress or the BJP does not face any difficulty while sitting with different groups and parties in a coalition government. Class interests are a binding factor among all parties and groups because commonality of class approach can be a cementing factor for groups which project disparate ideologies. Foreign policy of India, and liberalization and globalization of Indian economy have become a unifying factor of public policy package pursued by coalition of multiple class strata either led by the BJP or the Congress.

Mr. Kumar of Shipra's and Mr. Kuldeep Kumar of the Office of the Distinguished Scholar of JNU, New Delhi have made every effort to bring this study in the shape of a book. Thanks to Mr. Kumar and Mr. Kuldeep.

JNU, New Delhi
October, 2009

Chandra Prakesh Bhambri

Contents

1

Introduction: Coalition or Fragmentation of Politics

Every practitioner of bourgeois democratic political theory in India has suggested, even disserted, that the withering away of the Congress dominance over the whole political system after ruling for forty years of post-Independence phase of democratic politics has brought to an end the system of dominance of any single party over the Centre and the states of India. The Congress phase of political dominance has ended and it has been replaced by a coalition system of governance at the level of central government. It has also been argued that the emergence of the coalition system of governance at the Centre is also integrally linked with the rising assertions and aspirations of regional and sub-regional political groups and regional identities. It deserves to be clearly stated that the Congress itself was a coalition of classes, communities, and multiple socio-cultural identity groups and the cementing factor to this coalition was provided by an all-India Congress party ideology and organizational apparatus. The first short-lived coalitional system of government at the Centre was in 1977 and this experiment came to an end in 1979. The context of 1977-79 coalitional experiment should be kept in mind because it was first time in the history of post-independence India that the Congress party was decisively defeated in the elections and replaced by a coalition government at the Centre. Indira Gandhi's infamous, even notorious, Emergency Regime of 1975-77 was rejected by the voters of India and political parties, groups and leaders, who had opposed such an emergency regime, were brought to power by the voters on an anti-Emergency Regime Platform. The internal disputes and personality clashes among the leaders of 1977-79 Janata government at the centre rocked the boat and the verdict of Lok Sabha elections of 1979 was in favour of

Indira Gandhi Congress. Indira came back to power after a brief exile of two years and in 1984 Lok Sabha elections, the Congress secured three-fourth of the Lok Sabha seats. It was surmised that the Congress had come back to occupy old status of dominance over the Indian political system but it proved short-lived because Congress governments remained in office at the Centre from 1980 to 1988 and in the 1989 Lok Sabha elections, the Congress was reduced to the status of single largest minority party and VP Singh with minority support replaced the Congress and he became Prime Minister with the '*Outside*' support of the BJP and the Communists. This 'freak' arrangement made VP Singh proclaim that he was an expert in the 'management of contradictions' and manage the Central Government. VP Singh's so-called self-proclaimed expertise of 'management of contradictions' failed to keep him in power even for one year and this experiment of coalition government collapsed and the Lok Sabha elections of 1991 provided an opportunity to the Congress led by PV Narasimha Rao to form a government with only 220 out of 543 Lok Sabha members. It deserves to be mentioned that short-lived VP Singh-led government 1989-1990 had created and intensified social conflicts and cleavages based on caste versus caste politics, the Narasimha Rao government from 1991 to 1996 had divided the country on 'religious basis' because the government completely failed to face the challenge of Hindu communalism of the Sangh Parivar. VP Singh's Mandal politics, and Narasimha Rao's failure to confront 'Mandir-Masid' politics of the Sangh Parivar are legacies of weak and vacillating governments which were based on very limited political legitimacy. The VP Singh and the Narasimha Rao governments of 1989-90 and 1991-1996 could not or did not want to face socially divisive demands because their governments had very limited electoral support and legitimacy. A socially divided India of the 1990s began its political journey which has been described by bourgeois practitioners of political democracy as the era of coalition governments at the Centre and the emergence of the phenomenon of regionalization of political process. The coalition phase of politics at the Centre has seen VP Singh, Chandra Shekhar,

HD Dev Gowda, Inder Kumar Gujral, Atal Bihari Vajpayee and ManMohan Singh as Prime Minister from 1989 to 2009. The forty years of Congress dominance had Jawahar Lal Nehru, Lal Bahadur Shastri, Indira Gandhi, Rajiv Gandhi as Prime Ministers, and the withering away of the Congress dominance over political system gave birth to a galaxy of Prime Ministers some of whom do not have any place in the footnotes of Indian politics.

What is the evaluation of coalitional era of governance at the Centre based on the criteria of governmental performance? The supporters of coalition government at the Centre have argued that the Congress dominance over the country had led to the 'centralisation of power' and the state governments had become mere applicants and supplicants to the Centre, and coalitional system of government has led to the re-federalization and decentralization of power and a proper balance of power has emerged between the Centre and the States. This has been claimed as first positive consequence of the change from Congress dominance to coalition governments at the Centre. The second positive development of coalition system of government has been seen in the process of new consensus making in democracy. It has been suggested by the votaries of coalition system that power sharing by many political parties and groups at the Centre has brought multiple social groups at common platform of decision-making and politics of accommodation has become institutionally possible because many parties and groups sit together to decide about governmental policies. It has been suggested that coalitional system of politics has broadened the social base of democratic decision-making processes in India.

The critics have maintained that multiple groups decide to join a coalitional government with the sole purpose of controlling the levers of power and there is nothing in common which binds diverse heterogeneous groups to come together and from a government. The Vajpayee-led coalitional government at the Centre from 1998 to 2004 had consisted of members of the BJP and practitioners and believers of Hindu Rashtra and this government led by the forces of Hindutva was sustained and maintained from 1998 to 2004. The co-existence of die hard Hindu Communalists and secular pretenders cannot be described as the phenomenon of de-ideologization of Indian politics because Atal Bihari Vajpayee's party in the coalition did not abandon its core ideology of Hindutvan and Hindu Rashtravad. The real explanation is that irrespective of ideological antagonisms, coalition government was formed because diverse groups were interested in the exercise of governmental power for the sake of power. The ManMohan Singh-led coalition government from 2004 to 2009 was maintained and sustained by the 'outside' support of more than sixty members of the Communist parties. This marriage of convenience or inconvenience came to an end when the Communists decided to withdraw their 'outside' support from the ManMohan Singh government on its pro-American foreign policy and Nuclear Agreement between India and the United States. When the Communists withdrew their support, a vote of non-confidence was moved against the government in the Lok Sabha and the ManMohan Singh government survived the vote of non-confidence because the loss of votes of the Communists could not adversely affect the government because Mulayam Singh's Samjavadi party decided to extend its support to the government. The government survived because one supporter withdrew its consent and another new supporter consented to standby the government. The Fifteenth Lok Sabha elections of May 2009 brought rich political dividends to the Congress and its allies and ManMohan Singh became Prime Minister for the second time and formed a coalition government at the Centre in 2009. Congress and its allies have been always engaged in a tug of war from 2004 onwards because every group in the coalition is busy in maximizing benefits for itself, its social constituency, and its leaders in the Lok Sabha. Every groups in the coalition government is involved in pushing its own specific, special and local interests even at the cost of national interests. These are two sides of collation experiment in India and practitioners of bourgeois democratic political theory have highlighted its positive and negative features but on the whole, they are supportive of coalition system of government at the Centre.

Marxist Perspective

A scientific theory for the study of society provides an important 'key' or an 'entry point' for grappling with complex and contradictory social forces and processes which are at work at a given historical phase of development of society. Marxist Scientific Theory's greatest contribution is that any study of complex an contradictory web of social relations cannot be undertaken without linking social relations with existing material forces of production in society and any concretization of productive forces is possible only by identifying the nature of property relations which exist in society. the ownership of private property is then an instrument in the hands of the class of owners to appropriate social surplus value which is produced by the working classes and these class relationships between the expropriators of surplus value created by the toiling working classes determines the reality of power relations in society. A society which is divided into classes of private property owners and the real producers of wealth leads to the concentration of real 'power-social-to-economic-political and cultural' in the hands of private property owners who create institutions for governance and exercise of power over the exploited classes and power to exploit is exercised by the state power which is controlled by the real ruling classes in a society. The struggle for capturing power of the state in democracy is reduced to the struggle between two unequals i.e. the class of appropriators of surplus value and the majority of labouring classes who are the real producers of wealth. Thus the real issue is: Who controls the State in class-divided societies? Politics as an activity in class-divided societies is an area of struggle between the antagonistic classes and state control by the dominant classes provide them with an opportunity to exercise their power supported by the state for exploitation of the labouring classes.

The contemporary Indian situation is that 'coalition governments' are reflective of political fragmentation of various strata of the exploiting propertied classes whether industrial capitalism or surplus producing peasant classes. The various strata of the exploiting classes are politically organized either around weak all-India parties like the Congress and the BJP or locally dominant exploiting groups have politically organized their local, regional and sub-regional parties and group sand these diverse and multiple parties and groups, whether all-India or regional/local do not find any difficulty to 'join' together and form a coalition government. The Indian ruling exploiting classes do not feel threatened by any powerful challenge from their antagonistic exploited labouring classes and in such a historical situation, multiple strata of the exploiting classes have a field day to compete among themselves and maximize benefits for themselves by controlling the levers of state power. India is witnessing 'political tensions' among various strata of the ruling classes and these tensions are resolved by fighting elections against one another and form a coalition after the verdict of elections. The Communist parties of India have formed United Left Front to oppose the politics and economics of the ruling classes and the message of their ideological battle against imperialism, capitalism and exploitative landlordism is confined to West Bengal, Kerala and Tripura. The Communists exercise an all-India influence without al-India power. Another challenge to the ruling classes and its every strata has come from Maoist Liberation groups who have taken to armed struggle against the state of the ruling classes. The Indian state has strengthened its armed forces to deal with Maoist Guerilla warfare and the Maoist struggle and state response is just leading to 'deaths' without any social goal.

The Central issue for any Marxist practitioner of politics is to launch people's struggles with a view to transform their 'social consciousness' which is at the present limited by caste-based consciousness or religion-based consciousness or region-local based levels of awareness of social reality. The Indian masses are still tied with pre-modern social-cultural categories like caste or sub-caste and religion. Every strata of the ruling classes is engaged in solidifying the pre-modern loyalty structures of the struggling masses and in such a situation 'coalition of the exploiting groups' have a field day and they do not feel threatened by any large scale 'mass action' by the millions of deprived in society. This is the class reality of India. The ideological superstructure is influenced, even determined, by the cultural categories of historical past and political battles are fought on the basis of mobilization of caste versus caste or religion versus religion. Divided and disunited labouring classes can not pose any threat to the ruling exploiting classes, and the so-called coalition politics of India has emerged as a successful model of political contest among the exploiting groups. The most telling example of the coalition of multiple strata of the exploiting ruling classes is that a broad consensus on economic path of development and foreign policy has always existed among them. The India of 1990s and the first decade of the Twentieth Century has operated on the basis of broad consensus among the diverse strata of the coalition of exploiting ruling classes by following pro-imperialist, pro-American policies based on the model of free market-led competitive capitalism. The model of economic and pro-imperialist policies followed by the BJP-led coalition from 1998 to 2004 was also followed and full continuity of policies was maintained by the new coalition-led by the Congress from 2004 to 2009. The Communists of India were kept out of coalition of the exploiting ruling classes whether led by the BJP or the Congress because they had stood for an alternative model of independent foreign policy and demanded abandonment of the policies of free market-led competitive capitalism. The Communist parties have remained on the margin of political power system because they had led an opposition to the model of policies pursued by coalitions of the multiple strata of the exploiting classes.

How does one explain the co-existence of broad consensus on policy framework of 'coalition of the ruling classes' from 1990 to the end of the first decade of the Twenty First Century, and at the same time the existence of fundamental ideological divide between 'secularism' and 'Communalism' in the country? If on the one hand, an important segment of the ruling coalition of classes proclaims an ideological commitment to 'secular model of modernization of society' on the other, an equally significant segment of the ruling exploiting classes openly advocate the establishment of Hindu Rashtravad. The secularist along with Hindu Rashtravadis share common ideas on pro-imperialism and privatization and globalization of Indian economy, on the other, they are poles apart on the basis issue of the role of religion in politics of multi-religious and multi-cultural society.

The upshot of above narrative is that the coalition system of governance at the centre has been studied from different, even opposite, theoretical perspectives and the narrative in this study can be analysed, explained and evaluated by the readers on the basis of their preferred theoretical approaches. The narrative deals with concrete responses of coalition government to specific public issues which have faced this country.

2

Party Politics: National

Constitutional Legacies of the Country are Sacrosanct; Its Opponents are Committed to a Questionable Definition and Idea of India

Prafull Goradia, an ideologue of Hindu *rashtravdis*, in his article, 'Flaws in the legacy' (February 6), has found basic defects in the philosophical and conceptual postulates of the Indian Constitution and pleaded for changing it completely. Goradia holds the Constitution responsible for the day-to-day failures of proper and efficient governance in the country.

He says the root of most of our problems lies in the unimaginative mindset of the Constitution-makers who ignored differences between 'Hindu ethos' and 'Judaic tradition' which seem to have influenced them because 'the makers plumped for the Government of India Act, 1935'. He suggests that Hindus believe in the freedom of every devotee to choose his own path. Judaic priority for equality too does not hold the interest of a Hindu whose spiritual preference is for liberty.

The better the *karma*, the greater is the *bhagya* and vice versa. The believers of Brahminical ethos of hierarchical Hinduism have always maintained that the Constitution represents alien or foreign cultural ethos and this is the reason that it should be reframed and rewritten to make it relevant for serving the interests of Hindu ethos. The advocate of this ideology represents a school of thought and this is the reason that his arguments are being subjected to scrutiny for refutation.

The framers of Constitution were subjected to criticism from many schools of thought during the process of its making. First, the Hindu Mahasabha, Ram Rajya Parishad and MS Golwalkar of the RSS et al had castigated the makers for ignoring Hindu values by accepting foreign ideas and incorporating them into the Constitution. The representatives of Hindu ethos believed that Hindu *rashtra* could be defined as 'one culture, one nation and one country'.

MS Golwalkar had stated that for such 'one Hindu country', the Constitution should make the President very powerful. He also said linguistic reorganisation of India posed a threat to national unity. The Sangh Parivar defined Hindus as a 'monolithic' cultural entity and linguistic-cultural multiple identities were not only rejected by the believers of 'one Hindu *rashtra*', these cultural diversities of India were even considered a threat to national unity.

The Constitution makers not only rejected such definition of Hindu *rashtra* based on monolithic conception of Hindu ethos, they also accepted that the Constitution must establish unifying institutions for the governance of a highly diverse society from Jammu & Kashmir to Kanyakumari.

The definition of Hindu religion and *rashtra* as propounded by VD Savarkar and others was completely rejected and an alternative definition of India was incorporated into the Constitution. It is not only an abstract and definitional difference of opinion between the mainstream philosophical perspectives followed by the Constitution makers and the votaries of Hindutva because the Sangh has consistently targeted 'non-Hindu' Constitution.

It is not without reason that the BJP-led NDA Government at the Centre between 1998 to 2004 seriously considered 'altering' the Constitution and replacing it by incorporating Hindu ethos as understood and defined by the Sangh Parivar. The BJP-led Governments at the Centre and in several States have been engaged in teaching the impressionable students about 'Hindu values' with a view to subvert the secular constitutional ethos.

The point to be clearly understood is that Goradia and others of his ideological persuasion are not waiting for re-writing of the non-Hindu Constitution, but are continuously active and engaged in the indoctrination of children in schools by teaching them so-called Hindu values.

The cat jumps out of the bag when Goradia says that 'Hindus' spiritual preference is for liberty' and he praises anachronistic concepts like *karma* and *bhagya*. How does the Sangh deal with problems created by the Constitution with which it has fundamental philosophical differences? The Sangh has followed three strategies to erode the foundations of philosophical values underlying the Constitution.

First, after taking the oath of office, Government powers are used to promote Hindu interests and ideologies with a view to distance Hindus from Muslims and Christians.

Second, the Sangh tries to inculcate Hindu values among the students by using a BJP Government's power and control over educational institutions. Education in India is a part of the concurrent list and State Governments have immense power over educational institutions. Sangh Parivar ideologues are actively involved in promoting Hindu values in education under the protective umbrella provided by the BJP-led Governments.

There is nothing wrong if Governments promote secular, democratic and pluralist cultural values through education because such an agenda is in conformity with the Constitution. The difficulty arises when the constitutional powers are exercised to promote values which are contrary to the spirit of the Constitution.

Third, the Sangh Parivar has used past and present BJP State Governments' powers by enacting laws which are primarily against Muslims and Christians – the telling examples of such anti-minorityism are 'anti-conversion laws' passed by the State legislatures. The Fundamental Rights in the Constitution provide religious equality to all citizens.

Besides, Indians have the fundamental right to preach their religions and if a citizen is unwilling to practice a particular faith, he or she, by implication, has a right to abandon his or her religion of birth. Why should a citizen not be given the choice to abandon or follow one or the other religion? The anti-conversion law is like the sword of Damocles used by biased and partisan Governments of Hindus to target minorities.

The upshot of the above description is that our constitutional legacies are precious. Hindu *rashtravadis* are committed to a fundamentally different definition of India from the one provided in the Constitution. Hence the Constitution, as it is, has to be defended. A warning should be issued against turning it into a political football, particularly by transitory political groups because historically, it is always the temporary usurpers of power who have subverted constitutions. *13 February 2007, Pioneer*

Quota Blowback

The Pandora's Box of reservation has been reopened by the violent agitation launched by the Rajasthan Gujjar Sangharsh Samiti. The Gujjar community in Rajasthan, till now classified as OBC, is up in arms against the Vasundhara Raje Government, demanding it be reclassified as Scheduled Tribe. The Gujjars believe they will benefit more from reservation under the ST category than as OBC.

The ongoing struggle of the Gujjar community has reopened the contentious issue of caste-based reservation in public institutions. All political parties have promoted caste-based reservation for winning elections on the basis of a guaranteed support from a specific social constituency. The best illustration of political consensus on the policy of extensions of caste-based reservation in public institutions is provided by the 93rd Constitutional Amendment on the basis of which a parliamentary law has been enacted in 2006 to provide 27.5 per cent reservation to OBC candidates in Union Government-aided institutions of higher learning.

The policy of caste-based reservation has become an instrument in the hands of politicians to win over caste-based support. During the last 60 years, the process of including more and more castes in the category of reserved category has become an unstoppable phenomenon, thanks to unique political consensus on the issue. Every political party is deeply involved in it. Former Prime Minister VP Singh played this game in August 1990 when he announced the acceptance of the Mandal Commission's report, recommending quota for the backward castes in public services.

The logic of reservation is at work. The Vasundhara Raje Government is caught in a difficult situation. If the demand of the Gujjar community is accepted, her political opponents will instigate some other caste group for some other demand. If politicians are the originator and patroniser of a contentious and extremely divisive political problem, solutions have to found by them.

Another irrefutable argument against caste-based reservation has been provided by the Supreme Court while hearing an appeal against the implementation of reservation of seats in the Educational Institutions Act, 2006, by asking the Government about the deletion of 'creamy layer' from the category of reserved seats. Incidentally, the apex court had prohibited the 'creamy layer' category for reservation in public services while hearing a case against the Mandal Commission recommendations.

The policy of reservation is, in reality, not meant for the needy, deprived and economically handicapped social groups, but for the elite among the castes described as 'backward'. The backward strata of society deserve special concessions, attention and financial aid to come out of their low economic status.

It is the duty of a democratic state, especially in a country of great inequalities, to undertake specific public policies by targeting the really economically and educationally deprived sections of society. Public policies should be formulated to uplift the poor from their existing status of deprivation by opening special schools for them. Besides, a public policy based on a scheme of scholarship for primary, secondary and higher education is needed.

Tamil Nadu is the headquarters of the reservation policy. The major Dravidian parties are even against the limit of 50 per cent reservation of seats, as decided by the Supreme Court. They want an amendment to the Constitution to remove any ceiling over percentage of quota in public institutions.

Tamil Nadu has been ruled by powerful 'intermediate castes' for the last 40 years. These castes, while in power, have been extending the scope of reservation for their own caste fraternity. It is not without reason that the DMK, alongwith 'backward caste' leaders of Bihar and Uttar Pradesh, have been spearheading the movement for OBC reservation in education institutions.

Caste-based reservation is a logical extension of cast-based politics. The consequence of this phenomenon is that Indians society is completely fragmented. Today, Gujjars are just following in the footsteps of Jats. Policy of reservation has institutionalised the caste system because Governments have put their seal of approval on multiple caste identities.

Caste-based reservation creates a monolith category of a specific caste, while the reality is that such a category is artificially constructed by politicians. The poor cut across caste or communal lines and do not get benefits of reservation because the creamy layer of every caste grabs the benefits of reservation. The elite is the real beneficiary of reservation. *4 June 2007, Pioneer*

Politics of Regression

Not very long ago, the BJP Government in Rajasthan faced a serious challenge posed by a casteist movement. The Gujjar-Meena clashes in that State brought into focus the pernicious role played by caste-based mobilisation in the country. It will be interesting to analyse this episode, along with Ms Mayawati's strategies of building a caste coalition in Uttar Pradesh, besides paying attention to caste politics in Tamil Nadu.

Rajasthan's story is interesting. The BJP tried to win over Jats – the traditional vote-bank of the Congress – by granting them 'Other Backward Caste' status. Jats of Rajasthan were neither poor nor deprived. Since Jats were included in the OBC category, Gujjars, who had been in the OBC category, felt threatened. As a result they started demanding the Scheduled Tribe status for themselves. Thus, the BJP landed up in this difficult situation of having to resolve such a tricky issue where the interests of one caste are in conflict with that of another.

The BJP's difficulties got aggravated when the Meena community, who were already included in the ST category, strongly opposed to the inclusion of any other caste into this 'privileged' category. They were just not ready to share the benefits of reservation with them.

As far as Ms Mayawati's success in Uttar Pradesh is concerned, it is quite instructive as the commentators went overboard about her 'electoral strategies' missing the point that the State has further sunk into casteist politics. The argument is that Ms Mayawati succeeded because she had formed a 'rainbow coalition' comprising many castes, yielding rich political dividends. It must be mentioned that any post-election analysis based on electoral results reveals only a tip of the iceberg, as politics is a complex phenomenon.

Further, it has often been stated that the socio-political structure of Uttar Pradesh has been completely shaken by the awakening of the backward castes and the Dalits. The process of political churning, which began from the mid-1980s, has also led to an alternation in the social structure in the State.

The era of Brahmin-Thakur Chief Ministers – Govind Vallabh Pant, Kamlapati Tripathi and VP Singh – is over. In the new phase, OBC Chief Ministers like Mulayam Singh Yadav or Dalit leader Mayawati have emerged. Hence it is not for the first time that Ms Mayawati or Yadav have won elections.

What has been the impact of this 'social churning' on societal relations in Uttar Pradesh? Has the emergence of these erstwhile subordinate castes on the centre-stage of State politics resulted in social awakening among the weaker sections of society?

Answers to these questions will help us gauge the nature and quality of political change taking place in Uttar Pradesh. It can be unambiguously stated that the Dalits feel secure and empowered under Ms Mayawati's regime. Her rise has added to the confidence of the Dalits, who had suffered at the hands of higher castes in the past. No wonder they identify themselves with Ms Mayawati.

This is just one side of the story. In spite of the fact that power has been transferred to the OBCs or the Dalits, the level of consciousness in society is only restricted to identifying with one's caste or sub-caste. Even leaders are identified as caste leaders. Every leader in Uttar Pradesh during the past 60 years has mobilised a particular caste constituency with a view to confront another. Is it the meaning of social churning in Uttar Pradesh? Worse, caste-based reservation and political mobilisation have gone hand-in-hand to perpetuate casteism in society.

While Uttar Pradesh happens to be a 'backward' state', Tamil Nadu has been ranked as a 'developed' one. In spite of differences in the levels of development between the two States, Tamil Nadu's politics is no less casteist.

The dominant backward castes of Tamil Nadu – Thevars, Vanniyars, Nadars, among others – have their own political groups. These castes have ruled the State for over 40 years. Atrocities committed on Dalits by these followers of Naicker have to be seen to believe. Since castes and sub-castes have to be patronised, Tamil Nadu has the distinction of granting 69 per cent reservation in public institutions.

The conclusion of above analysis is that Ms Mayawati's electoral success or Tamil Nadu's claim to progress cannot stop the strengthening the caste system. After all, caste-based politics perpetuates casteism and lays firm foundation for the strengthening of caste consciousness. An alternative secular politics cannot be born unless the people are liberated from the inherited legacy of caste by birth. 2 *July* 2007, *Pioneer*

Rethink Reservation

On August 8, the Supreme Court was in no mood to provide any relief to the Union Government. Instead of passing an interim order, it decided to pursue the discussion on the Central Educational Institutions (Reservation in Admission) Act, 2006.

Incidentally, the UPA Government assured the court that if the withdrawal of 'reservations given to the creamy layer among the OBC' was a stumbling block, it was ready to exclude them from the category of reserved seats. The apex court, however, rejected the offer and decided to continue with the hearing of all the issues involved with this new quota policy in educational institutions of higher learning maintained by the Centre.

Such an opportunity provided by the Supreme Court can be fruitfully utilised to have a wholesome 'relook' on the issue of caste-based reservation in the country. The Act of 2006 has provided caste as the sole criterion and basis of reservation for Other Backward Caste (OBC) students in institutions of higher learning. It is a well-known fact that the policy of reservation for the OBCs has nothing to do with social uplift of the poor. In fact, the provisions of the 2006 Act are miles away from any concern for social justice and equity in society, especially in the field of higher education.

A little demystification of the construction of the concept of OBC is essential to understand the real motives behind the unstoppable caravan of reservation. A powerful backward caste peasantry has emerged since the mid-1960s and every political party has been striving hard to accommodate this new assertive class.

The middle class peasantry was the first to walk out of the Congress's umbrella platform. This led to the weakening of the country's grand old party. Meanwhile, the OBC peasantry – from Tamil Nadu in the south to Uttar Pradesh and Bihar in the north – have formed their own 'regional-caste-based parties.

Incidentally, castes like Jats or Yadavas and many others in the OBC category are neither the victims of social discrimination nor are they poor. After all, they belong to the class of surplus-generating peasantry. The caste-based discrimination is a reality in India, but it should never be forgotten that at least the OBC peasantry is not its victim.

In reality, it is Dalits (untouchable Shudras) who are being subjected to tyranny and exploitation by the newly empowered peasant castes. The new exploiting and oppressing castes are getting the benefits of new policies of reservation of 1990 and 2006.

The above narrative shows that caste-based reservation is a demand of the powerful intermediate peasantry and its political leadership and has nothing to do either with caste-based discriminations or programme for the uplift of the downtrodden.

The country's political power is in the hands of OBC leaders who, in turn, patronise their own caste groups.

It does not require any expert to suggest that the patronisation of caste by politicians has led to caste versus caste and sub-caste versus sub-caste rivalries and conflicts. It is not only in Rajasthan that incidents like Gujjar-Meena violence are taking place; growing caste rivalry has, in fact, become a reality of India.

Caste-based privileges have led to the phenomenon of casteism and social fragmentation. Every specific caste or sub-caste has created its own political shop and political competition has been reduced to caste competition. The adverse impact of growing casteism in politics has been felt on governance. Many State Governments are unstable as they are being ruled by opportunistic alliances in which every representative of caste-based specific constituency is claiming share in public institutions.

The upshot of above narrative is that our political parties or leaders have completely fragmented society and the policy of reservation has institutionalised the caste system in India. In the process, it is the poor people who suffer and the governance becomes a casualty.

It is time we abandoned caste-based reservation policies for uplifting the upwardly mobile backward peasantry. Instead, efforts should be made to improve the conditions of the real Shudras, who should be brought into the centre stage of governance. *14 August 2007, Pioneer*

Frequent State Assembly Elections Shift Focus from National Issues

No matter how much we celebrate the infallibility of our democracy's institutionalistation of free, fair and competitive elections, we must also be apprised of the weaknesses in the system. All regional and national parties are regularly engaged in electoral battles either for the Lok Sabha or State Assemblies. Imagine the spate of elections we have had in the recent past and those that are going to be witnessed in the near future. Every major political party was involved in the elections for the Assemblies in Punjab, Uttarakhand, Uttar Pradesh, Gujarat and Himachal Pradesh in 2007. In 2008, 10 State Assemblies have to be elected. By the time the next Lok Sabha election is held, expectedly in 2009, there will be more State Assemblies that will have to be elected again. The Congress and the BJP will spend the whole of 2008 fighting Assembly elections in Karnataka, Madhya Pradesh, Chhattisgarh, Rajasthan, Delhi, Jammu and Kashmir and also in the North-East (Tripura and Nagaland). In this scenario, all-India parties are unable to project a national agenda because of their engagement in continuous electoral battles that are regional. They are expected to shift their focus on purely local issues every now and then.

During the Assembly election of 2008 in Rajasthan, for example, the State's voters will not only be concerned about the performance of their State Government, but also agitated on the local issue of reservation on caste basis involving Gujjars, Meenas, Jats and all. Both the Congress and the BJP will have to respond to the issue cautiously. This may but have national implications as well. Then in Karnataka, HD Deve Gowda, a maverick political operator who matters mainly to his State only, will force local issues on the electorate and national parties will have to compete against the agenda of the JD (S).

The Lok Sabha election of 2004 was a contest between two national slogans – 'India shining' versus 'neglect of the *aam aadmi*'. Unfortunately, the BJP and the Congress, who had raised those national issues in 2004 were forced to speak only on regional issues in most State Assembly elections of 2005, 2006 and 2007; the story is likely to be repeated in 2008.

When the BJP-led NDA Government decided to include Jats in the list of OBCs in Rajasthan in 2004, it was a telling example of a national party abandoning its all-India policy in favour of a local demand. The BJP accuses the Congress of Muslim appeasement with a view to win elections, but it forgets that it too has followed a similar policy – that of sectarian appeasement.

Now take the issue of fund raising for elections. Say, the

Trinamool Congress or the BSP collects funds to fight elections in West Bengal or Uttar Pradesh, respectively, while the BJP and the Congress need to accumulate huge resources to compete against two dozen major State-based parties that collect resources only for their own State elections.

If the Prime Minister and his Cabinet of Ministers are continuously engaged in electoral exercises from Tripura to Jammu & Kashmir, as will happen in 2008, the work of governance at the Central level is bound to suffer as national agendas are sacrificed at the altar of regional politics.

The root cause of this evil system is the delinking of Lok Sabha and State Assembly elections of 1971 and 1972 by the Indira Gandhi Government. The elections of 1952, 1957, 1962 and 1967, with general and Assembly elections both finishing within a span of two months, were held in a manner that national leaders talked of national agendas during election campaigns and State-level leaders and party organisations looked after local issues.

The British election system has not proved suitable for the Indian federal system but the American system can act as a good guide. In the US, elections are held simultaneously for President, the House of Representatives and Governors for many States every four years. This not only saves time, energy and resources of political leaders, but Americans are also able to discuss State-specific issues with a national perspective during Presidential elections. America's federal system, centred around the President and Governors, can be moulded to suit India's parliamentary democracy.

India should be liberated from the continuous cycle of elections so that parties can focus their attention on governance instead of getting distracted by one election after another.

Horold J Lakshi in his classic, *Parliamentary Government*, stated that elections are held to form a 'Government' as well as an 'Opposition' so that the former is kept on its toes. Prof Lashi did not visit India to find that elections have become a national pastime and neither the ruling party nor the Opposition has any time to perform the basic tasks of democracy. 31 *January* 2008, *Pioneer*

Before 'Discovering' India, Rahul Gandhi must 'Discover' his Party

Congress general secretary Rahul Gandhi's recent visit to Orissa has attracted a lot of attention, thanks to his bold statements. He said that the Congress will be run 'democratically' and the prevailing '*lalbatti* culture' will be brought to an end. 'One of my main purpose is reducing the distance between politicians and the people. I have to be close to the people', he further added.

Gandhi's agenda is to 'democratise' the functioning of the Congress and replace its culture of 'high command' by making the functioning of the party transparent. His wishful thinking reminds us of the statement of his father, Rajiv Gandhi, who wanted to cleanse the Congress from the shackles imposed by party stalwarts acting as 'power brokers'. Gandhi needs to be reminded that his father's agenda remained a non-starter because he had no understanding of party politics.

Rajiv Gandhi had a smooth journey within the party till his mother, s Indira Gandhi, was alive. The story about his gradual downfall after the assassination of Mrs Gandhi substantiates the argument that he did not have any understanding of party politics. The so-called loyalists of Mrs Gandhi turned against him; the story may repeat itself for Rahul Gandhi if his mother, Ms Sonia Gandhi, falters. Hence Gandhi, instead of 'discovering' India, should discover his party.

Further, Gandhi, while 'discovering' his party, should look at the reality which emerged during the Gujarat Assembly election. Narendra Modi campaigned as 'the leader and sole spokesman of Gujarati identity', while the Congress did not have any local leader who could match Modi. How can the party confront its political opponents without regional leaders.

Worse, the Congress has the record of reducing its defeated leaders to insignificance. Digvijay Singh of Madhya Pradesh, Ashok Gehlot of Rajasthan and Amarinder Singh of Punjab have been marginalised in their States after party lost the election. How can it think of coming back to power if it treats its leaders disdain. If a former Chief Minister cannot lead the party after its defeat, he should not have been party's candidate for chief ministership.

If Ms Gandhi has not been able to build effective organisational structure at the State-level, Gandhi has not shown any capacity or understanding of the party's internal factional politics. If the Congress has to send Priya Ranjan Dasmunsi or Suresh Pachauri from the Centre to strengthen the State party organisation, it shows the bankruptcy of its organisational structure at the grassroots level.

The Congress has not learnt any lessons from its defeats in State Assembly elections. When the BJP defeated the Congress in Himachal Pradesh, the party replaced its Chief Minister with another leader. Karnataka is the best example of the Congress's failure to learn any lesson from its electoral defeats. SM Krishan was removed after the party's defeat in Karnataka and sent to Maharashtra as Governor; months later he has been brought back to Karnataka to confront the Janata Dal (S) and the BJP. The upshot of this narrative is that Gandhi has no strategy to strengthen the party in the States.

The Congress can face political challenges only by strengthening its party organisation in all the 25 States. It needs regional leaders with significant mass following. Gandhi, before 'discovering India', needs to comprehend the logic of multi-polar politics and party system of the 21st century.

The upshot of above narration is that Gandhi has not emerged as a leader in Congress; at the present, he is operating under the umbrella of his mother. His discovery of his own party will be revealing because 'loyalists' to Ms Gandhi need not continue as faithful and dependable supporters of her son. This is the crux of the issue.

Gandhi has not been able to create a viable and strong party structure. He is depending on his mother for his political survival.
19 March 2008, Pioneer

Courtiers are not Masses

A politically correct approach can be taken on the issue of 'dynastic culture' flourishing in the country, particularly in the Congress, by stating that it is purely an internal matter of a political party to select or elect any leader for the post of Prime Minister or Chief Minister. Further, a political party is expected to elect its own leader by following democratic procedures and the controversy surrounding the proposal that Rahul Gandhi should be the prime ministerial candidate of the Congress has been generated by well-known courtiers – Arjun Singh and Pranab Mukherjee.

It deserves to be stated that the Congress has followed the tradition of nominating – and not electing – its leader. And the criteria of selection is one's accidental birth to a 'special' family. It can further be stated that it is purely an internal matter of the Congress to follow dynastic politics.

Thankfully, things are much better in the country than those in Pakistan. Benazir Bhutto, unlike the followers of dynastic politics in India, decided to 'write her own will' and handed over power to her son after her death.

An important question remains: Is Indian democracy safe in the hands of politicians who violate democratic norms in their parties? The answer is that dynastic politics and democracy cannot go together. This is the first significant reason to deplore the dynastic tendency of the Congress, along with many other regional parties, to project sons and daughters of their leaders as future Prime Ministers or Chief Ministers.

The greatest advantage of democracy is that political leaders and their views and actions are known to the people, thanks to the media, both print and electronic, besides the efforts of the Opposition to bring out in public the mistakes of the Government.

Ms Gandhi, as Congress president between 1998 and 2008, has established herself as the undisputed leader who has succeeded in saving the sinking ship of her party. She has been critically analysed by the media and the Opposition. In the process of these 10 years, she has been accepted as the undisputed leader of her party.

In contrast, what are the contributions of Gandhi in strengthening his party organisation? What are Gandhi's political credentials to occupy – or even be considered for – the office of the Prime Minister of India? He is yet to prove himself.

First, Gandhi has not achieved any electoral success for his party. The first test for him, as Congress general secretary, came during the Gujarat Assembly election. He, however, failed miserably to create any impression on the voters in favour of his party. The political presence of Gandhi during the Gujarat election held after his nomination as general secretary made no difference as far as voters are concerned; the party was defeated in the State.

The second test for Gandhi has been revealed by his complete failure to turn the tide against Ms Mayawati, whose social base remains intact despite his much publicised visited to Dalit families. If on the one hand, Gandhi has not made any impact on the minds of the voters, on the other, he has not made any political statement either.

Mrs Indira Gandhi had a tough time between 1966 and 1969 and she came on her own when she electrified the country by raising the slogan, 'Garibi Hatao', against her opponents' slogan of 'Indira Hatao'. Mrs Gandhi vanquished her opponents in the 1971 Lok Sabha election on the basis of her political platform and message. A 'dumb doll' emerged as a leader in her own right on the basis of her political message.

Gandhi has not given any meaningful political message and till today he seems to be confused and confounded. He has to learn about the complexities and contradictions of Indian politics. During his learning process, it is wrong to project him as the prime ministerial candidate.

It will be a great disservice to Gandhi and the Congress to push such a novice to the centrestage of power politics. First, he must understand the intricacies of power politics before aspiring to become Prime Minister. *20 April 2008, Pioneer*

Quota doesn't Help Dalits: Traditional upper caste oppression has been replaced by OBC tyranny

The Dravadian political leadership, which has always boasted about its 'rationalist' belief system, must be embarrassed – even humiliated – when a wall separating Dalits and the backward caste of Thevars and Venniyars was demolished by Tamil Nadu Police on May 6. It is ironic that the inheritors of a 'rationalist' ideology have been practising the policy of segregation, even apartheid, by constructing a wall, which blocked the common pathway. This incident shows that Dalits are not equal to the other castes.

It deserves to be mentioned that the so-called socially progressive DMK-led coalition Government was compelled to demolish this wall because one political party threatened to 'launch an agitation if the wall was not brought down by May-end'. There is no reason to believe that the Dravadian political parties would have, on their own, felt that the wall separating Dalits and other castes was an act of humiliation for the whole society. After all, the wall was demolished by the Government under threat of agitation from a national political party.

Tamil Nadu, irrespective of its inheritance of anti-Brahmin movement, continues to be a casteist society. The purpose of above narrative is to highlight the fact that Tamil Nadu's cultural life is not different from the much-maligned Hindu heartland. If Thevars indulge in atrocities against Dalits in Tamil Nadu, Jats of western Uttar Pradesh have never hesitated in doing the same. The Ministry of Home Affairs released a report on May 4, saying, 'In 2006, 4,960 cases of crimes were committed against Dalits in Uttar Pradesh. At least 4,214 cases in Madhya Pradesh and 3,891 cases were registered in Andhra Pradesh'.

It should be stated that village tyranny against Dalits is not fully reported. An appreciable step was taken when the Scheduled Caste/ Scheduled Tribe (Prevention of Atrocities) Act, 1989, was put on the statute book. It is an established fact that the land reforms undertaken by the Government after independence had led to a shift of power from the traditional high castes like Brahmins, Rajputs and Bhumihars to intermediate land-owning backward castes.

Land reforms only displaced the traditional high castes and replaced them by land-owning middle/peasant castes. Oppression against the most vulnerable Dalits has been a continuing reality of the past 60 years, though with a difference: The old traditional oppressors have been replaced by the new oppressing castes.

A few analytical issues need to be addressed by keeping in focus the unchanging oppression against Dalits. First, the primary agenda of every Dalit party or leader, along with parties and leaders of OBCs, has been for extending the sphere of reservation. Every caste-based political group has justified the demand for reservation on the basis of achieving the goal of 'social justice' for the historically oppressed castes.

Caste system is not an all-India system because caste is a local or sub-regional phenomenon. It was artificially constructed as an all India phenomenon when VP Singh implemented Mandal Commission recommendations in 1990 and provided reservation at an all-India level. This was the first attempt to give a local phenomenon an all-India colour.

The UPA Government, following the example of Singh, has provided reservation for OBCs in India's premier education institutions. Is there still any ambiguity that caste-based reservation is meant to promote 'social justice'? Or is it a reflection of the growing clout of OBCs in Indian society?

Thus, caste-based reservation has nothing to do with social justice. Reservation has institutionalised caste divisions in India and has promoted casteism in society. India has become a full-fledged caste-based society because every political party has promoted caste or sub-caste-based interests through reservation. Is it surprising that caste-based conflicts and violence have become a phenomenon in Indian society?

If political parties are interested in pursuing pubic polices for catering to the interests of their caste constituencies, then Dalits can face greater discrimination in future. After all, the weaker the caste group, the greater will be chances of it being oppressed. This is the explanation for continuing caste atrocities against Dalits in Ms Mayawati's Uttar Pradesh or 'rationalist' M Karunanidhi's Tamil Nadu.

The policy of reservation has only strengthened the hold of powerful OBCs over state apparatus. This is the reason why OBCs do not hesitate in committing crime against Dalits.

Reservation has not brought any advantage to the poor. If we are serious about breaching the wall of separatism among castes, we must learn from other countries. Since politics of caste and the policy of caste-based reservation have led to the assertion of caste-based identities, a wall of separatism among various castes is a logical phenomenon. The caste versus caste competition leads to social distancing among people. Tamil Nadu is the centre of caste-based reservation; no wonder, the worst form of untouchability is being practiced in that State. Even the place of cremation of the dead is determined by caste-based identity.

Reservation in public services has contributed to the growth of social separatism in India. Reservation has facilitated the growth of social separatism in the country. So, is this policy of caste-based reservation worth pursuing? The answer is a big no. At least the well-wishers of Dalits should oppose reservation. 20 *May* 2008, *Pioneer*

Congress in Deep Trouble: It must allow its State leaders to grow in stature

The Congress, after dominating India's political landscape for more than 40 years since independence, is in deep trouble. It is unable to withstand the political challenge posed by its political rivals. It must be discomforting for the party to see its decline, even decay.

A few facts may be mentioned to substantiate the argument that all is not well for the Congress. First, the Congress-led UPA Government consists of multiple and disparate centres of power – from at least 14 regional parties to the Communists, who are its outside supporters.

The Congress is not leading the coalition; on the contrary, it allies are dictating their policies on the Congress-led Government. It can be stated unambiguously that the UPA is not a coalition but a caricature of a coalitional system of Government in which every group or party is able to push its own agenda and the Congress has to swallow the bitter pill.

Second, the Congress could rule India for so long because it had presence in every region, small or big, from Jammu & Kashmir to Kanayakumari. Its dominance has come to an end because it has been politically outwited by its political rivals. Moreover, the country's political geography has changed and regionalist or sub-regionalists are able to compete against the national parties; the Congress is the worst victim of the changing profile of State-level politics. The party is not only at the receiving end of the changing scenario; it has also to come to terms with regionalists for even its marginal political presence – from Tamil Nadu to Bihar and Uttar Pradesh.

What is the explanation for the Congress's failure to compete against powerful and not powerful regional forces? The Congress, or any other claimant to an all-India status, cannot win sizable Lok Sabha seats if it has a marginal or localised presence in one State or the other. Local political groups, masquerading as regional parties, represent sectional social constituencies and remain confined to limited area of influence, both socially and geographically. These 'local groupings' can succeed against all-India parties at local levels only if the State party structure of the all-India parties is weak and unable to politically challenge its opponents. The Congress has shown its political fragility because it has refused to accept that its State party leaders have to show political strength to compete against regional opponents.

The Congress does not allow its State leaders to grow; this stands in sharp contrast to regional leaders like M Karunandhi, Ms J Jayalalithaa, Prakash Singh Badal, Mulayam Singh Yadav, Lalu Prasad Yadav, or even Ms Mayawati, who stands at par with our national leaders.

The Congress does not project any one leader at the State level who would confront the leader of opponent party. Narendra Modi was a recognised leader of Gujarat, but the Congress did not have a competitor against him. The same story was repeated in Karnataka. While the BJP and the JD(S) projected their leaders during the Assembly election, the Congress did not known its mind. The telling example is SM Krishna, who had been the Chief Minister of

Karnataka. After the electoral defeat of the party, he was shifted to Maharashtra as Governor. Krishna was brought back to Karnataka a few months before the 2008 Assembly election to play an active role in campaigning for the Congress; he, however, was not found competent enough to contest the State Assembly election. Further, the Congress has to face tough State Assembly elections in Chhattisgarh, Madhya Pradesh and Rajasthan; and, in all these States, the local party workers are clueless about their respective State leadership.

Even the BJP is faction-ridden, but unlike the Congress, it adopts correctives before the election. It happened in the case of Himachal Pradesh where Prem Kumar Dhumal was declared the party leader and Shanta Kumar, another contender, was brought to the Rajya Sabha. The BJP settles factional disputes among its State level leaders, and the Congress shuffles and reshuffles the leaders and after every electoral defeat, its Chief Ministers are left in the wilderness.

What is the explanation for the failure of the Congress to evolve matching strategies of its opponents at the State level? Why is the Congress not taking any corrective steps at the State level? While the regional political parties have an advantage over the Congress because they are revolve around one personality; it does not mean that the Congress cannot find effective leaders in its party against sectarian, casteist and regionalist leaders. The real problem is with the phoney mindset of the politically bankrupt 'High Command'.

The Congress is mostly led by leaders at the Centre who cannot win elections on their own and the consequence is that they take wrong decisions regarding regional politics. *3 June 2008, Pioneer*

Media and Politics of Dynasty

The Indian media never fails to give a miss to anything about the children of Ms Sonia Gandhi, M Karunanidhi, Prakash Singh Badal, Mulayam Singh Yadav and Lalu Prasad Yadav, without realising that they are facilitating the phenomenon of dynasty in politics. In Anglo-American democratic systems, both the print and audio-visual media follow a self-denying ordinance of keeping out any trivial information about the progeny of Prime Ministers or Presidents or the Leaders of Opposition.

Sachin Pilot came out with words of wisdom on September 28, 2008 that Rahul Gandhi had all the capabilities of becoming the Prime Minister. Pilot forgot that he was not competent to make a political forecast about the fate of his own party after the Lok Sabha election in 2009. Prime Minister Manmohan Singh, on the other hand, stated on October 1, 2008 that it is too early to talk in terms of a potential Prime Ministerial candidate. The Congress has several leaders who are equally or better qualified than I am, he said. Singh knows it quite well that he owes his chair to the Congress president.

Incidentally, this is not the first time that a Congress leader has made such a statement about Rahul Gandhi. It is very easy to understand the desire of different Congress party leaders who wish to convey to Ms Sonia Gandhi that they are more loyal than the king and by proposing Rahul Gandhi's name, in season or out of turn, they want to ensure only their own bread and butter within Ms Sonia Gandhi's Congress. More often than not the reports of sycophancy in the Congress have been out in one way or the other. Vijaya Lakshmi Pandit had summed up this trait of the party leaders in a famous statement that 'Indira is the only male member in the Cabinet'.

Sycophants within the party who are projecting Gandhi as the future leader would not occupy any worthwhile space in the media unless the purpose is either to flatter Ms Gandhi or to keep in good humour the UPA Government. Further, the dynastic politics in India neither begins nor ends with the Congress at the Centre because every major non-Congress and anti-Congress regional party is also following in the footsteps of the Congress.

The Abdullahs and the Muftis are dividing the political space in Jammu and Kashmir. Sheikh Abdullah's grandson and Mufti's Mohammed Syed's daughter have been projected by their family chiefs as the young face of Kashmiri politics and the media, both at regional and national level, have never questioned the right of inheritance.

Mulayam Singh Yadav, a self-appointed backward caste socialist does not see his Uttar Pradesh-based party beyond his brothers and son while Ms Mayawati, not to be left behind, has proclaimed publicly about her chosen inheritor in politics. The vernacular media in the State prominently projects the family inheritors of politics of Mulayam Singh Yadav and Ms Mayawati. HD Deve Gowda used every trick of the trade to make his son Chief Minister of Karnataka and the media projected him as a great secular Opposition leader against the present BJP Government. A great rationalist and an atheist, Karunandhi, and a large section of the media in Tamil Nadu, controlled by his family, are working over time to distribute his political inheritance to his sons and daughter.

Karunandhi's dilemma is that his children are claimants to the post of Chief Minister which they want to inherit from their father. It may be conceded that a country can have political families like Pratap Singh Kairon, Devi Lal or Govind Vallabh Pant *et al*, and successful parents have every right to allow their children to be in active politics. But the issue is: Are the offices of Chief Minister or Prime Minister reserved for a family or a dynasty?

The voters of India did not repose their confidence in the Sonia Gandhi-led Congress and from 1998 to 2004 the Congress stayed in the Opposition. The story thus far is quite normal but the twist in Congress politics began with the media, out of the blue, portraying Rahul Gandhi for the highest office in the country without rhyme or reason.

It must be very embarrassing for Prime Minister Manmohan Singh that even before the next Lok Sabha election is scheduled, he has been put on notice by a coterie of sycophants in the Congress which is projecting Ms Sonia Gandhi's son as Prime Minister-in-waiting. *3 October 2008, Pioneer*

India under Siege

The prime minister, at the end of his foreign visit, had to publicly admit on September 28, 2008 that the ongoing violence against the

Christian community was a matter of great 'national shame'. And on his arrival in Delhi on October 1, the central government decided to convene the 14th meeting of the National Integration Council (NIC) on October 13 to evolve a national consensus on the serious threat which was faced by minority communities in secular India.

The central government brought all CMs including the BJP leadership on a common forum of the NIC to make everyone agree and recognise that 'unity and diversity and communal harmony constituted the bedrock of 'our nationhood' and these 'civilisational values' have to be 'effectively defended' by political parties and central and state governments'.

It deserves to be clearly stated that continuous efforts have to be made to protect and defend the secular fabric of Indian democracy because the 'composite culture' of Indian plural society has always been challenged by the believers and practitioners of 'mono culture Hindu Rashtravadis'. It is not an accident that during the ongoing violence against 'minorities', RSS chief K S Sudershan, writing in Organiser stated that 'Muslims want to convert the whole world to Islam and the Christians want to see the whole world as followers of Christ'.

It deserves to be recalled that Jawaharlal Nehru, who was conscious of fissiparous tendencies in a diverse society, created the NIC in October 1962 with a view to bring all political opinions on a common platform to face the challenges to the unity of a diverse society.

The central issue is that the NIC meeting of October 13 has been held at a time when not only anti-minority political forces are actively engaged in targeting the life, property and places of worship of the minority communities, but also at a moment in the post-Independence history of democracy that the central government is not ready to take on the anti-minority forces with all the powers given to it by the Constitution. Can there be any relevance or meaning of the 'national consensus' arrived at by the NIC meeting without concrete governmental intervention in the alarming prevailing situation of communal disharmony and discord?

First, the central and state governments have to identify ideological groups which are openly or in a clandestine manner engaged in spreading hatred and violence against minorities. It deserves to be stated that the Students' Islamic Movement of India (SIMI) is a fundamentalist organisation and a ban has been imposed on its activities in 2002. The judiciary has been involved in getting to the bottom of the truth about SIMI.

Ideological training of SIMI members makes them Muslim religious fanatics who can spread hatred and violence against other religious communities of India. On the other hand, the Hindu fanatics are no different. As VHP secretary and former Bajrang Dal convener Surrendra Kumar says, 'Veer Savarkar's Hindutva is our ideological goal.

Hindutva is not a form of worship. It is a political term. Everyone who considers India his Pitribhumi (fatherland) and Punyabhimi (holy land) is a Hindu and Indianness is the same as Hindutva' and Islam and Christianity are 'out of Hindutva' as they are 'foreign to Bharat'. The Dal and VHP have implemented their 'political ideology' of anti-Muslim and anti-Christian Hindutva and their active role in anti-minority activities has been visible in public.

A national daily reported on October 14 that 112 people have died in 22 communal clashes in the past two months in the country. It is also an accepted fact that the Dal and VHP have been actively involved in the recent killings and burning of Christian churches in Orissa, Karnataka, Madhya Pradesh and Rajasthan. *13 October* 2008, *Economic Times*

Declining Political Capability

The logic of a globally interdependent age demands that effective collective global interventions be made for finding solutions to the international financial crisis. But leaders and managers of each and every national political system in the world must find solutions that are specific to their respective countries. For, the government of a democratic country cannot afford to blame the financial crisis, which is being experienced by its citizens, on 'global factors'.

Prime Minister Manmohan Singh had stated as early as October 24 that 'we cannot remain totally unaffected...our stock markets and the exchange rate of the rupee are under pressure due to capital outflow of foreign institutional investors'. He had further admitted the rate of growth in India would slow down because of the international ambience. Commerce minister Kamal Nath is on record that India's exports have declined because of the economic crisis faced by the developed capitalist countries. However, the Indian political system, including both political parties and institutions of governance, is simply proving incapable of providing any coherent road map or blueprint for dealing with the grave challenges that our economy and society are facing.

A few facts may be mentioned to substantiate the argument that politics has proved itself not worth much in dealing with the crisis at this juncture. First, the authority of the central government to provide a coherent all-India policy perspective has been completely eroded and the Congress-led UPA government has shown that every single group within the coalition is pursuing its own agenda. Every single group is concerned with maximising its electoral gains by championing one or the other 'local' issue with an eye on its local constituency.

The agenda for dealing with critical national problems has become subservient to the politics and agenda of localism. It is not only the UPA constituents which are working at cross purposes, the erstwhile supporters of the coalition, the Communist parties, have never lost any opportunity to oppose and criticise economic and foreign policies pursued by a government, which they had supported from outside. Mulayam Singh's Samajwadi Party, too, has a similar story.

The SP is not only supporting the UPA from outside but is also engaged in keeping the Manmohan Singh government on tenterhooks by its criticisms on the Batala House encounter incident or Amar Singh's tirades against telecom minister A Raja, whom he has accused of pursuing the telecom policy in a manner that enables him to favour a 'chosen' few among corporates. How can the

Manmohan Singh government, in such circumstances, provide any effective political leadership during this grave crisis?

Second, a crisis situation demands an across-the-board 'political consensus'. The UPA cannot make the BJP and the Communists, two major opposition formations in the Lok Sabha, to agree even on a minimum economic programme for dealing with the serious crisis that India faces. Opposition parties have taken their role to oppose the government too seriously and any hope of even a 'round table' conference between the government and the opposition groups for arriving at some minimal consensus on policy interventions is currently not at all possible. 20 *December* 2008, *Economic Times*

Impart Secular Education

President Barack Obama, like every other enlightened secular Democrat, has understood the critical role of 'education for secularism' in his fight against religious fundamentalism. Obamaâ•™s public action should alert Indian policymakers that religion-based ideology in public life cannot be challenged without compulsory education where schools have a scientific and secular curriculum. Post-Independence, we have failed to lay the foundation of a structure of educational system which would help in the growth of enlightened citizenry. The failure of the government has led to large-scale privatisation of education. Muslim madrasas and Hindu rashtravadi-affiliated Shishu Niketans and other are taking advantage of it, especially in the tribal belts of Rajasthan, Madhya Pradesh, Chhattisgarh, Orissa, Jharkhand and Bihar. The teaching of Islamic theology and especially the Holy Quran is the basic agenda of Muslim seminaries/madrasas. Similarly, the RSS-affiliated network of schools is engaged in promoting Hinduisation. The Sachar Committee on minorities has reported that about four per cent of Muslim children attend madrasas. The government of India, instead of being worried about the cultural growth of Muslim children on non-secular values, has come out with a 'centrally-sponsored scheme for providing quality education in madrasas (2008-09)'.

Not only this, the government will give recognition to the certificates issued by the state madrasa boards, and they will be treated as equivalent to CBSE certificates. How can a secular state give legitimacy to an educational system based on theology? The government, both at the Centre and the states, must establish primary and secondary schools throughout the country.

It is an obligation of secular India to create public educational network with a view to completely eliminate the need or justification for the existence of non-secular and unscientific educational institutions like madrasas and RSS-affiliated Shishu Niketans. Further, these theological or quasi-religious educational institutions should be completely debarred from any public funding, recognition or approval.

Further, the textbooks prescribed and taught in these educational organisations are spreading religious hatred. Centre is thinking of countering this by establishing National Text Book Council. This idea is not acceptable to many state governments, especially BJP-led states. The National Council for Educational Research and Training (NCERT), involved in the writing of textbooks for schools should be a non-government 'autonomous' council managed by professionally-qualified educationists. There is a great need for autonomy of the NCERT so that it can produce scientifically-written secular textbooks for schools. Act before it is too late and make NCERT autonomous. *31 December 2008, Asian Age*

Wishful Thinking: Can government, opposition work in harmony?

The 15th Lok Sabha seems to have begun its journey well because the two major parties, the Congress and the BJP, have made a public commitment that Parliament will function in a constructive manner and the working relationship between Government and Opposition will be based on mutual respect.

The statements made by Prime Minister Manmohan Singh and the Leader of Opposition in the Lok Sabha, LK Advani, as well as his counterpart in the Rajya Sabha, Arun Jaitley, clearly show that

Parliament is expected to operate according to the best traditions of democracy where Opposition is not treated with contempt by an arrogant majority party and where relationship between majority and minority parties is based on mutual understanding.

Advani has assured the Government that the Opposition will not be found wanting in extending cooperation to the Government on issues of national interest.

It will be a great mistake on the part of the Manmohan Singh Government to ignore the observations made by the Opposition because it binds the Government to arrive at a national consensus on domestic and foreign policies. In his reply to the debate on the President's address to Parliament on June 9, Manmohan Singh asked for a 'bipartisan approach', especially on issues relating to development and national security.

The question is: Keeping in mind the history of animosity and hostility which has existed for a long time between the parties in power and those in the Opposition, is it possible for them to work together? It has also been suggested that politics of consensus-making can flourish and exist only in societies where political parties have fundamental agreement on national problems and such a reality is found only in the democracies of the West.

National consensus on issues relating to the security and welfare of the country is not possible in a conflict-ridden and ideologically divided society. How can political parties agree on any national interest issue when they have fundamental differences among themselves on matters of national development?

The first glimpse of the collapse of consensus was seen in the very first session of the 15th Lok Sabha on the Women's Reservation Bill. Not only this. Major political parties have very different perspectives on the policies of economic reforms even when the world is facing a deep and prolonged recession. Do all the major parties agree with Singh's view that it is in India's 'national interest' to develop normal relations with Pakistan?

Further, the Trinamool Congress and the DMK, allies of the Congress in the UPA Government, have voiced their opposition to the proposed policy of disinvestment in public sector undertakings, and as the process is begun, many Opposition parties will also come out against it. Arun Shourie of the BJP has already given a hint of opposition to disinvestment in public sector units.

Also there seems no agreement among parties on national security issues. Any major terrorist attack leads to sharpening of differences between the Government and the Opposition. After the 26/11 terrorist attack on Mumbai, the BJP has been demanding stringent laws to tackle the problem while the Government has shown little enthusiasm in this regard.

A very ticklish issue in India is the relationship between party/ parties in Government at the Centre and the State Governments ruled by parties in the Opposition. For example, Ms Mamata Banerjee of the Trinamool Congress will keep the pot boiling in West Bengal in her anti-Communist crusade. While trying to do so, she will likely demand support from the Congress-led Union Government. Or, for that matter, a BJP-ruled State will not easily accept a Congress-appointed Governor if there is a conflict between the Chief Minister and the Governor.

The CPI(M) is leading a revolt against the Governor's decision to allow the CBI to frame charges against its own party leader in Kerala. It is unlikely that the Congress will not appoint its own favourites as Governors and it is impossible to expect the Opposition parties not to suspect the actions of such Congress nominees. Many BJP State Governments have been at loggerheads with Congress-appointed Governors; it is too much to expect the Congress to behave differently with non-Congress State Governments. Will there be no conflicts?

Then it goes beyond saying that the Government and the Opposition may have a minimalist common programme for governance, but the points that divide them are more fundamental than what brings them together. Harmony between the two seems to be wishful thinking. *19 June 2009, Pioneer*

No Smooth Sailing for Congress

After the results of the general election that saw the Congress winning 206 seats and marked the party's comeback to power, its allies seemed quite dwarfed against the grand old party. Unfortunately for the Congress, its moment of glory was very short-lived as it was compelled to eat the humble pie by its alliance partners after forming the Government.

A very ugly face of political brinkmanship was seen when DMK chief M Karunanidhi descended in New Delhi with a list of party candidates for ministership in the new Manmohan Singh-led Government. Not only did he decide the number of ministerial posts for his kith and kin but also decided the portfolios that they would get.

It is legitimate for an alliance partner to bargain for a number of ministerial berths in the Cabinet, but the distribution of portfolios to Ministers is the sole prerogative of the Prime Minister in a parliamentary system of Government. But this was not the case. This time it was not Singh calling the shots but Karunanidhi while the Prime Minister was simply asked to put the seal of formal approval on it.

The story does not end here. Union Railway Minister and Trinamool Congress chief Mamata Banerjee, another ally of the Manmohan Singh Government, in her enthusiasm to play the Opposition in West Bengal simply ignores the fact that as a Cabinet Minister she is bound by 'collective responsibility' of decisions taken by the Council of Ministers. When the Centre asked the Left Front Government to impose a ban on the Maoists in West Bengal and decided to deploy paramilitary forces, a furious Banerjee came out against the decision and instead asked her party's Ministers in the Central Government to visit Lalgarh.

Again, when the Centre announced an increase in petroleum prices on July 1, Ms Banerjee was the first Cabinet Minister to flay the decision publicly. One wonders whether Ms Mamata is in the Opposition or in the Government?

By maintaining silence over the recent disclosure by Justice R Raghupathy that a Union Minister had sought to influence him in a case relating to the grant of advance bail to Dr C Krishnamurthy and his son Kiruba Sridhar, Prime Minister Manmohan Singh exhibits the ugly compulsions of coalition politics. This is the worst example of political helplessness.

The above happenings raise some fundamental questions about the functioning of coalition Governments in general and the present Congress Government in particular.

Gone are the days when political parties lent support to the party forming the Government considering some essential commonality. Today it is the benefits that come along with the office and not the ideological commonality that brings parties to form the Government.

The emergence of coalition politics has provided oxygen to small regional political parties who, with a limited support base from a specific region, have come to the centrestage of politics without any sense of national responsibility. Regionalists have not outgrown their localism and sense of parochialism.

It will be premature to suggest that the coalition Government at the Centre will have a smooth ride ahead because the its regional allies do not seem to show any intention to reconcile local interests with those of national. *8 July 2009, Pioneer*

Tackling Maoists: Red terror must be crushed ruthlessly

Union Home Minister P Chidambaram's statement in Parliament on July 15 that more people died in violence linked to Maoist insurgency during 2008-09 than in insurgent attacks in North-East India is alarming. It is equally alarming to note that the Maoists have spread to 150 districts in the country. The Government should not turn a blind eye to the capacities which Maoists have built by playing with the emotions of the marginalised and neglected sections of the society, especially in tribal belts.

Prime Minister Manmohan Singh and Home Minister P

Chidambaram have identified Maoists as the greatest security challenge confronting India. Admitting that India underestimated the Maoist threat, Chidambaram also recently said in Parliament that the threat has grown because challenges posed by it were not dealt with seriously and effectively by the Governments, both at the Centre and in the States.

The maintenance of law and order is the responsibility of the State Governments under the Constitution, but if law and order problems cut across State boundaries and if nine States and 150 districts are badly affected by this, the Central Government has to play an active role because coercive apparatus and paramilitary forces of the country are under the control and supervision of the Central Government.

It should be clearly understood that strategies of involving local population to fight against well-armed Maoists is based on a completely wrong understanding as they are well-equipped to take on the might of the State and it happened in Lalgarh during anti-Maoist operations in West Bengal. Although the anti-Maoist operation in Lalgarh succeeded in bringing an end to the Maoist presence in that area, the West Bengal State police forces and the Central Paramilitary forces failed to arrest Maoist leaders as the escape routes to Orissa were available to the Maoists.

This is the reason that made Chidambaram state in Parliament that concerted anti-Maoist operations were never launched in the past and in the atmosphere of policy confusions, Naxalism had grown.

Unfortunately, former Union Home Ministers could not make up their mind about the real meaning of the Maoist problem. Many a time, they termed it a social problem but did nothing to tackle the social causes that were leading to the problem. At times, previous Home Minister Shivraj Patil said that Naxalism is a challenge against the law and order of the state and should be met with heavy hand by the police forces. However, unlike his predecessor, Chidambaram has his task cut out. He seems to have made up his mind that he will follow the policy of 'bullet versus bullet' and make his police forces well-equipped to deal with well-armed Maoist groups.

While Chidambaram is prepared to catch the bull by the horns, it remains to be seen whether State Governments have a meeting of minds with the Home Minister.

Time has come to take the fight against Maoists to their den. But at the same time it is important to keep in mind the betterment of the socially backward people. Affected States should chalk out plans for upliftment of the tribals. To an extent, the rise of Maoists can be traced into the state failure in uplifting the social and economic status of the poor and backward tribals.

It is myopic to think that Maoists can be eliminated without silencing their guns and ignoring the basic needs of the poor in the affected areas. *21 July 2009, Pioneer*

Not Just a Question of Rhetoric

The Congress party has come to occupy the leading position within the UPA coalition government at the Centre. Unlike the 14th Lok Sabha where the Congress had only 156 seats of its own, it has emerged as the centre of power in the 15th Lok Sabha with 206 seats of its own in the House of 543. It deserves to be underlined that the pro-aam-aadmi agenda of the Congress is not based on any rhetoric. As Sonia Gandhi stated at the meeting of the Congress Parliamentary Party, the voters of India have renewed their confidence in the party because of its socially inclusive and pro-poor developmental philosophy of governance.

A political party in a democracy does not survive on the basis of its old achievements or moments of electoral glory. It has to perform for its survival and future electoral victories and the Congress party is not an exception to this general rule. The commitment of the Congress party led by Sonia Gandhis to India's future was clearly and unambiguously reflected in the annual budget of 2009-10 presented by finance minister Pranab Mukerjee. A few salient features of the annual budget indicate the direction towards which the country may be moving under the new UPA-II government.

It is for the first time in the history of post-independence India that an annual expenditure of more than Rs 10 trillion has been proposed in the budget. Second, rural India, i.e., Bharat, is the focus of investments and the special focus is on the farmers and the poor. While farmers have been given an 'interest subsidy', the NREGS, the flagship programme of the Congress party, has received an amount of Rs 39,000 crore, an increase of 144% from the budget of Rs 16,000 crore of 2008-09. Third, the focus is on Bharat Nirman, the rural housing fund, road connectivity, et al. The budget which is a political policy statement of the government is clearly focused on expanding the rural domestic market by creating purchasing power among the rural people.

India had begun its journey of planned economic development on the basis of an assumption that the benefits of economic growth will have a 'trickle-down-effect' and pull the people out of poverty. The new vision of the Congress party seems to be that it is only the 'bottom-up, socially inclusive approach' which will bring the 300 million or so people out of their existence below the poverty line.

The UPA government in its first term had launched the bold programme of NREGS. In its second avatar, the UPA government is taking the next step in the direction of welfare of the real poor in the form of the National Food Security Act. The government, on the basis of a parliamentary legislation, has decided to guarantee the supply of 25 kg of rice and wheat at Rs 3 per kg to the 'rural and urban poor'. Jean Dreze, the eminent liberal economist, has stated that 'the proposed right to food Act can be a solid complement to the NREGS'.

While the right to employment to the rural poor is a prerequisite to create a sense of 'self-esteem and a feeling of dignity', the right to food is a must for survival.

Is it fair to maintain that the overall philosophical perspective of the Congress and the concrete budgetary allocations made by the finance minister provide enough evidence to characterise the Congress as as a left-of-centre party? The left-of-centre approach towards governance is not foreign to the Congress party's thinking. It should not be forgotten that Jawaharlal Nehru's real legacy is the left-of-centre Congress party. Indira Gandhi also wore the mask of leftism as a tactic to confront and confound her opponents within her party.

Strong voices have been raised against the rural poor-oriented policies and budgetary allocations. Such pressure groups exist within and outside the Congress. No doubt, Sonia Gandhi has to manage contradictory pressures or lobbies which are operating against its socially inclusive growth policy. It is worth noting here that the communist parties can play a constructive role in support of the new social and economic policies especially those that are pro-poor and pro-rural development.

How can the Left not support NREGS? The Food Guarantee Act has been a demand of the democratic and leftist parties. The communists have already suggested that instead of the government's proposed scheme of 25 kg at R 3 kg to the poor, their own preference is for the Antyodaya scheme which gives 35 kg of foodgrains at Rs 2 per kg to those below the poverty Line. The Congress party and the communists can resolve this issue and make a grand success of the pro-poor food security Act.

This budget has taken the first bold step in focusing attention on rural economic growth. With pressure from socially progressive groups, the government can be pushed further to generate more 'purchasing power' in rural India. Though a centrist party like the Congress can always be pushed around by the Left or the Right depending on the role of various political forces which exist in the country, the Food Guarantee Act can become a pillar of the party's left-of-centre politics. *1 August 2009, Economic Times*

Politics of Social Sectarianism

The language used by Uttar Pradesh Congress chief Rita Bahuguna Joshi on July 15 and the political response by Chief Minister Mayawati to Ms Joshi's intemperate language clearly show that 'democracy by dialogue and dissent by reasoning' does not exist in the State. Politics of dialogue based on arguments in Uttar Pradesh is conspicuous by its complete absence from public life.

This is in uttar contrast with the belief that democracy is a system of governance where political participants are always actively engaged in dialogue and discussion on pubic issues and critics and political dissenters are able to freely argue their case with a view to arrive at a consensus on public issues.

Ms Mayawati herself is guilty of using language in public affairs which cannot bring any credit to any leader of a party or a Chief Minister of a State. More often she has targeted Mahatma Gandhi by using language which, to say the least, has been derogatory. Her latest contribution to anti-Gandhian vocabulary is that Gandhi was a 'natakbaz' and his concern for Dalits was a 'sham' and a 'drama'.

Incidentally, neither Kanshi Ram nor Ms Mayawati know about many other social reformers who fought against the evil of untouchability in society. It deserves to be clearly stated that it is historically wrong to maintain that only BR Ambedhar had fought for the cause and rights of the untouchables. Ambedkerites like Ms Mayawati need to be reminded of the historical context in which Gandhi fought for the rights of the Harijans (Dalits) when British colonial power was dividing the Indian society on the basis of caste.

British rulers patronised Ambedkar during the Round Table Conferences of the 1930s and Gandhi undertook fast unto death and compelled the rulers to give reservations to the Harijans under the Gandhi-Irwin Pact. This description is necessary to set the record straight because Ms Mayawati has developed a habit of debunking Gandhi by choosing and using language which is not appropriate for any decent public discourse.

The larger analytical question is: Why has the level of public discourse and political culture in Uttar Pradesh sunk so low that dialogue is conducted in an idiom not worthy of the status held by leaders who are using these languages in politics and vitiating the atmosphere of public life?

Public life before and after independence in Uttar Pradesh saw constitutional debates in Legislative Assembly and struggles against colonial rule closer than most.

Men of letters like Munshi Prem Chand and institutions of culture like universities and colleges had contributed immensely to the overall cultural life of the State including politics. If one comes out of the nostalgia of the past, the deterioration has to be explained on the basis of overall political development of the State. An explanation which deserves to be completely rejected is that the present state of lack of political civility in the State can be attributed to the emergence of the politics of 'sub-altern classes' which has replaced 'elite politics' of the past. This explanation is unsustainable because the whole burden of deterioration in the standards of democratic debate has been shifted to the shoulders of the emerging Dalit and Backward Castes.

The focus is on the public conduct of leaders and not on the masses, and almost every political party and its leaders have contributed to the existing vitiated political culture in Uttar Pradesh. The growing trend of sectarian social divisions has given birth to an atmosphere of 'hate' and 'violence' against one another in the society. Ms Mayawati's often-repeated statements like 'Manuwadis' and her every attempt to create caste-versus-caste cleavages, an effort fully joined by Samajvadis like Mulayam Singh has completely fragmented society and created a social milieu of one against the other on the basis of an enemy syndrome in society.

The deepening social sectarianisation in Uttar Pradesh has led to the overall backwardness of the State and the prevailing political culture represented by Ms Joshi, Ms Mayawati and others is a mere reflection of this. Not only this, the State has been trapped into a vicious circle of overall socio-economic and socio-cultural downfall which does not surprise one given the deterioration and vulgarisation of political idiom in the State. In these circumstances, even a civilised democratic dialogue cannot be initiated, leave all-round progress. 6 *August* 2009, *Pioneer*

UPA's Drought of Governance

The media, the votaries of policies of economic liberalisation and privatisation of industrial and financial sectors of economy were hopeful that unlike the previous UPA Government, which was hamstrung by the presence of the Left, the Manmohan Singh Government in its second term would push further the policies of economic reform and liberalisation. But they were made to eat humble pie as all their hopes from the Government in power from the end of May to the middle of August have been completely belied.

The lacklustre performance of the Government in the first quarter of its second term is because of its incapability to provide meaningful leadership on national and international issues facing the country. Moreover, this time the Centre cannot blame the Opposition parties for following any obstructive approach.

Although Finance Minister Pranab Mukherjee said in the Lok Sabha that the first Budget session was very constructive because unlike local or parochial issues, members of Parliament had devoted their attention on issues of national and international concern, Railway Minister Mamata Banerjee staged a walk-out in protest against Government's proposed law on Land Acquisition at a formal meeting of the Cabinet.

The walk-out by a Cabinet Minister proves beyond any shadow of doubt that the Congress-led UPA coalition Government at the Centre consists of 'disparate groups' which have nothing in common and this coalition does not have any agreed common agenda of governance for the country. It clearly shows that the Government is bound to work on the basis of 'ad hocism' in governance.

Besides infighting, Prime Minister Manmohan Singh invited trouble for his Government at Sharm el-Sheikh in Egypt when he issued a joint statement with Pakistan Prime Minister Yousuf Raza Gilani on July 16 delinking the terror from composite dialogue. It will be wrong to maintain that only the Opposition parties reacted strongly against the statement. A divided Congress Party, and the country's public opinion also became antagonistic to the stand taken by Singh while dealing with his Pakistani counterpart. A new Government which had already failed to make any mark on public affairs was faced with a shaky leader whose foreign policy came under scrutiny.

It was Singh who suggested that a 100-day agenda of every Minister should be placed before public to convey the message that the new coalition Government means 'business' and people should judge it on the basis of its performance. The very intention behind the idea first 100-day agenda was laudable because well begun journey of a Government leaves a very positive impression on the people's consciousness. But this dream of the Prime Minister has disappeared in the thin air because coalition consists of 'disparate groups' without any thing in common among themselves and also because of his own poor start in his first foreign policy intervention with Pakistan.

Prime Minister's philosophical approach towards continuous and constant 'engagement' with Pakistan is laudable because the logic of proximity cannot be wished away. History and geography have a determining role in deciding the level of 'bilateralism'; however, foreign policy decisions have to be taken keeping the sentiments of people in mind.

The Prime Minister was caught on the wrong foot not on the issue of his approach based on continuous dialogue with Pakistan but on the operationalisation of policy at this moment because Indian public opinion is not favourable towards Pakistan.

The net result of acts of omission and commission of the Prime Minister, who has come to power for the second time, is that the first quarter of his Government has shown a condition of drought in policy making for the whole country. *18 August 2009, Pioneer*

3

Regionalists and Coalition Politics

UP Refuses to Move Forward: Uttar Pradesh continues to leg behind others as no political party desists from pursuing casteist as well as communal politics

Uttar Pradesh has become a victim of its flawed understanding of the State's historical inheritance. Every intellectual, socio-cultural and political formation in the State is at peace with primordial and primitive identities belonging to its feudal and semi-feudal past. It is not only that Uttar Pradesh lives in the past, the process of its historical backwardness also seems to be unstoppable, as every political party is consciously pushing it backward.

The coming Assembly election in Uttar Pradesh has further activated the champions of inherited identities of the voters to play their games of farcical politics by appealing to caste and religion. It was expected that the Congress would project itself different from other backward-looking parties like the SP and the BSP. This hope, however, seems to have beem belied by Rahul Gandhi's recent political speech in the State. On March 19, he made an astounding statement on Babri Masjid saying, 'Had anyone from the Gandhi family been active then, it would not have happened at all'.

The implications of Gandhi's statement on March 19 deserve to be highlighted to evaluate the political and electoral agenda of the Congress. First, the statement on Babri Masjid is significant because the Congress has decided to disown its own history and put the blame on the then leadership at the Centre – Narasimha Rao. Second, the statement is an attempt to project the Congress as a party of every Indian and it conveys a clear message that it will politically fight against the socially backward and conservative forces in the State. How does one accept such declarations on their face value?

Caste-based contest has become the essence of politics of Uttar Pradesh and secular social identities of the poor, oppressed and exploited groups have paled into insignificance. Every political party in the State is committed to the perpetuation of caste-based identities. The candidates for the Assembly election are selected on the basis of caste arithmetic and calculations.

BSP leader Mayawati has nominated party candidates on the basis of their caste identity to compete against other caste-based parties like that of Mulayam Singh Yadav and Ajit Singh. The self-appointed guardians of Hindu identity have formed an alliance with the Apna Dal, which represents a specific caste in the State.

Hindutva and caste are two sides of the same coin and the BJP's alliance with the Apna Dal substantiates the argument that identity by birth continues to be a determining factor in Uttar Pradesh politics. The Congress in the State is in doldrums and it is seeking alliance with Ajit Singh, the practitioner of Jat politics. The BJP is projecting leaders like Kalyan Singh and Rajnath Singh to win over the support of their caste constituencies.

The guiding principle of every party is to nominate candidates on the basis of their caste-base and caste-appeal. The vicious hold of caste over the levels of consciousness is a reality of State politics.

In Uttar Pradesh, electoral politics is engaged in resolving historically experienced injustice and punishing those who seem to be associated with atrocities of the past. It deserves to be stated that the agenda of economic development is always linked with the aspirations of new social groups like the farmers, the industrial workers the professionals, et al. How can the State deal with the agenda of economic development by appropriating the symbols of the past?

It is sad that the election in Uttar Pradesh is not being fought on the issue of futuristic agenda. Instead, the focus is on caste arithmetic, temple, Ambedkar, among others. Caste and communalism, as reference points of politics, have been equated, even substituted, by projecting various caste and communal leaders. The Congress, on the other hand, can be accused of playing dynastic-cum-personality-oriented politics, as was evident from Gandhi's statement in Uttar Pradesh.

The upshot of above description is that politics in Uttar Pradesh has not moved away from medieval practices and the representatives of this backward past are leaders and political formations of the State. The 2007 Assembly election will only see the extension of Uttar Pradesh's loyalty and commitment to feudal tendencies and identities. The State, unfortunately, refuses to move forward. *2 April 2007, Pioneer*

UP Frozen in History: Caste politics cannot remove casteism from society

Political dust has finally settled down in Uttar Pradesh. Now the central issue that deserves analysis is the future development of the State under Ms Mayawati's Government. The first step in understanding future prospects of Uttar Pradesh after the May 11 electoral verdict is to identify the causes of victory and defeat, as perceived and pronounced by the contenders for power.

It deserves to be emphasised that the vanquished Samajwadi Party has retained its social base by getting 25.45 per cent of votes; it had obtained 25.37 per cent votes in 2002 and 21.8 per cent in 1996. Incidentally, Mulayam Singh Yadav had become Chief Minister not on the basis of his majority of seats but by breaking other parties, especially the BSP. He has not taken note of his own acts of omission and commission and has blamed the impeccable arrangements made by the Election Commission for organising free and fair election in a State known for booth capturing and other forms of physical intimidation.

Ms Mayawati's electoral victory has been explained on the basis of her new 'social engineering' and also by raising the issue of lawlessness in Uttar Pradesh. The BSP has increased its vote-share from 19.64 per cent in 1996 and 23.06 per cent in 2002 to formidable 30.45 per cent in 2007, obtaining 206 seats out of 402 contested Assembly seats. It seems plausible that Ms Mayawati's 'social engineering' has paid rich dividends in the election.

The real loser in the Uttar Pradesh Assembly election is the BJP. The party obtained 32.52 per cent of votes in 1996, which went down to 20.08 per cent in 2002. It has further declined to 16.93 per cent this time, with 50 seats in an Assembly of 402.

The Congress's performance remains dismal and static. The party secured 8.35 per cent votes in 1996, 8.96 per cent in 2002 and nine per cent this time.

Muslim voters play a significant role in Uttar Pradesh elections. Yadav has always boasted of his formidable support of Yadavas and Muslims, but Ms Mayawati's 'social engineering' strategy seems to have dented the Muslim support base of the Samajwadi Party.

It is often suggested that caste or religion-based politics in a competitive democratic electoral system gets delegitimised once the voter becomes literate and prosperous. Tamil Nadu and Gujarat are high on the 'index' of development. Tamil Nadu had witnessed a powerful anti-Brahmin movement in the name of 'rationalism'. Is Tamil Nadu free from the evils of caste-based politics? The answer is an emphatic no. Today, every Dravidian political group is an extension of one caste or the other. Besides, the State is the headquarter of ritualised religiosity.

It is a far-fetched idea to believe that in a socially backward State like Uttar Pradesh, the new confederation of castes will bring an end to the caste system and lead to social progress under the leadership of 'socially engineered' politics of Ms Mayawati. There is not even an iota of evidence to substantiate the argument that the BSP's new caste alliance will lay down the foundations of new socially progressive Uttar Pradesh.

Similar is the story of highly developed Gujarat. Gujarati society is socially very conservative, in spite of the fact that Gujaratis have been socially very mobile entrepreneurs and businessmen. The best example of Gujarati social conservatism can be seen on the issue of prohibition. Economic development, therefore, is not a precondition for social progress.

New society and politics cannot emerge without replacing the inherited categories of caste or religion. Every political formation has perpetuated the symbols of 'old society' by undertaking political mobilisation on the basis of caste versus case and religion versus religion. Ms Mayawati is a product of this kind of politics.

Uttar Pradesh is frozen in history and none of the major contenders for power can be seen as messiahs for establishing new social order in that State. Hence Ms Mayawati's electoral success is only a re-enactment of the old drama of politics. Caste politics cannot annihilate casteism from society. Uttar Pradesh is sinking in politics of non-issues. *21 May 2007, Pioneer*

Left with Little Choice

Communists are ideologically and politically anti-Congress and anti-BJP and their outside support to the UPA Government at the Centre is at best a marriage of convenience. Further, the Left's attempt to maintain an equi-distance from both the Congress and the BJP has created a situation where it could not play any role in shaping public policies at the Centre. In fact, it was only in 2004 that the Communists, as a part of the UPA coordination committee, came to occupy the centrestage of Indian politics. They agreed to support the UPA from 'outside' on the basis of a common minimum programme. Incidentally, it was for the first time in the history of post-Independence India that the Congress and the Left could arrive at some agreed programme for governance at the Centre.

Such an arrangement between political antagonists could not have been smooth. Recently, it has almost come to a dead end on the issues of Indian foreign policy pursued by the Manmohan Singh Government. If the Communists withdraw their 'outside' support, the Government at the Centre cannot survive and fresh elections for the new Lok Sabha will have to be held.

What are the political options available to the Communists if they go for mid-term poll? CPI(M) general secretary Prakash Karat has repeatedly stated that unlike earlier experiments of Left and Third Front politics, the new Third Front would have to emerge from 'common struggles' on 'common issues' among the associates for any future Third Front.

The decisive electoral defeat of Mulayam Singh Yadav in Uttar Pradesh has freed him to create a patchwork of 'non-Congress, non-BJP front', which was designated as the United National Progressive Alliance. A few footloose regionalists of Indian politics – Mulayam Singh Yadav of the Samajwadi Party, Chandrababu Naidu of the Telugu Desam Party, Ms J Jayalalithaa of the ADMK, Om Prakash Chautala of the Indian National Lok Dal and Prafull Kumar Mohanta of the Assam Gana Parishad – announced the formation of the UNPA.

The previous record of such groups clearly shows that they are primarily a collection of political opportunists who do not practice or profess any ideology. After all, Naidu, Ms Jayalalithaa and even Chautala were partners of the BJP-led NDA Government at the Centre between 1998 and 2004. So, what's their credibility?

The first significant political intervention of the UNPA was to nominate a Muslim as a candidate for the office of Vice-President. Is nominating a Muslim candidate enough to prove its 'secular' credentials in politics, or is it a mockery of 'secularism'?

The Communists, because of their anti-BJP and anti-Congress politics, will have to seek allies to influence public policies at the Centre. Is Naidu, who curried favour with then US President Bill Clinton during his regime as Chief Minister of Andhra Pradesh, a suitable partner for the Left? How could they work with Mulayam Singh Yadav who practiced 'crony capitalism' as Chief Minister of Uttar Pradesh? It is worth recapitulating the above narrative to substantiate the argument that Communist politics of 'equi-distance' from Congress and the BJP pushes it towards a motley crowd of regionalist, casteist and opportunist parties.

How does the Left operate in a multipolar party system? The Communists, like other political parties, cannot take a 'purist' ideological position because the logic of electoral results goes against any ideological rigidity of any kind. The regional parties have nothing in common with one another. Worse, their leaders have huge personal egos.

What are the options for Communists in such kind of multipolar party system? First, they can go along with any non-Congress and non-BJP front and try to influence policy-making at the Centre.

However, such a Government with this kind of political arrangement would not last long. The coalition experience since 1989-90 substantiates this argument. A Government at the Centre, which is formed on the basis of 'negativism', has a limited lifespan thanks to inner contradictions among the allies.

Second, the Left parties can support or oppose the UPA Government on specific public policy issue. This political arrangement is workable because the UPA and the Communists can agree or disagree on specific issues. The Congress and the Left can work together only on the basis of this model. Issues in politics are important and support or opposition to issues should be mainstay of Communist politics. Else, they would be compelled to ally with the 'opportunist', regional parties. At present, issue-based support or opposition is the best political arrangement between Communists and the UPA. *30 August 2007, Pioneer*

The Fear of BJP is Keeping Congress and Communists Together

It's a marriage of convenience between the Congress and the Communist parties. A pretension of co-habitation between the two political formations is continuing because 2008-09 is an election year for the Lok Sabha and 10 State Assemblies.

However, the so-called working arrangement between the Congress and the Communist parties has not succeeded in stopping the electoral victories of the BJP in Uttarakhand, Himachal Pradesh and Gujarat, and the Akali Dal-BJP combine in Punjab. This is the reason why the Communists are currently working on the formation of an anti-Congress and anti-BJP 'alternative'.

It is for the first time in the history of post-Independence India that the Congress and the Left parties have decided to work together at the Central level. However, any alliance between the two politically antagonistic forces is untenable because there is no ideological meeting ground between them. Moreover, in the 2004 Lok Sabha election, 54 out of 61 Communist MPs won the poll by defeating their Congress opponents.

Communists are not alone in opposing the Congress; there are others like Chandrababu Naidu of the TDP, Om Prakash Chautala of the Lok Dal, Mulayam Singh Yadav of the Samajwadi Party, among others. These parties joined hands to form the UNPA, which failed to live up to its expectations.

The Communists were earlier hesitant to extend any legitimacy to the UNPA. However, on February 11, CPI(M) general secretary Prakash Karat decided to spell out ideas for the creation of an 'Left and National Third Front Alternative'. He stated that unlike the UNPA or other 'fronts', the Left parties would not ally for 'just an *ad hoc* pre-poll arrangement' as they were interested in 'a cohesive front of like-minded parties' based on 'a minimum common consensus in approaches and beliefs'.

What are the prospects of the formation of such 'Left and National Third Alternative'? The 'front' is unlikely to emerge on the political scene because leaving aside the all-India parties like the Congress and the BJP, all regional formations have their own socio-political agenda determined by their social base. Political parties and groups, whether as individual contestants in elections or members of an 'alliance' cannot abandon their 'core' ideology.

Chandrababu Naidu, a likely member of the 'Third Alternative', will back liberalisation policies, which stand in sharp contrast to the policies pursued by the Left parties. The Communists may need the TDP, but Naidu does not gain anything from the Communists in Andhra Pradesh. Mulayam Singh Yadav has been trying to curry favour with the Communists, but in Uttar Pradesh, he is not dependent on them for electoral gains. Similar is the case of Chautala. The upshot of above narrative is that the Left parties cannot have a 'progressive' national alternative to the Congress and the BJP.

If 'ideology' guides Communists, regional parties cannot be expected to abandon their 'ideology'. Anti-imperialism is a pillar of Communist ideology, while Yadav and Chautala are devoid of any such 'intellectual' understanding.

The 2009 Lok Sabha election and the State Assembly elections in 2008 will witness straight contests among all-India parties like the Congress, the BJP and the Communists alongwith State-specific regional parties. Any alliance of parties at best will be just an electoral exercise and at worst an opportunist collection of power-seekers.

Further, the first *real* non-Congress Government at the Centre was led by the Janata Party between 1977 and 1979; it was supported by the Jana Sangh. The story was repeated when VP Singh enjoyed power as Prime Minister for 10 months between 1989 and 1990 with the BJP's support. The moral of the story is that every coalition Government at the Centre has to depend either on the 'outside' support of one of the all-India parties like the Congress, the BJP or the Left parties.

The logic of 'tripolar' politics rules out the emergence of any viable governing coalition at the Centre without the support of either the Congress or the BJP. This is the only choice before the country and the 'Third Alternative' will have to reckon with the presence of either the Congress or the BJP. *20 February 2008, Pioneer*

Wages of Regionalism

Raj Thackeray's demand to reserve 80 per cent jobs for sons-of-the-soil in Maharashtra's private sector clashes with the idea of India

The greatest challenge to the idea of India has been posed by Raj Thackeray, who wants to reduce 'North Indians' to the status of second class citizens in Maharashtra. His latest threat is to the thousands of private sector enterprises in the State to 'reserve' 80 per cent of jobs for Maharashtrians only. The track record of Thackeray is that he will forcibly enforce his idea on the private sector operating in Maharashtra.

It deserves to be stated that regional chauvinism is creating a situation of informal balkanisation of the country. Kannadiagas and Tamils get emotionally provoked against one another on river water disputes. The two communities were involved in a confrontation in the first week of April on the Hagenakkal Integrated Drinking Water Project.

The Kannadigas, not to be left behind, have asked for the boycott of Tamil movies in Karnataka. It is not the first time that regional chauvinism has led to confrontation between the two States. The Cauvery river water dispute has always been a bone of contention.

India is inhabited by multiple region-based cultural communities. The reorganisation of States in 1956 was based on the recognition of the fact that regional cultural diversities are a reality and it will help the cultural life of diverse communities flourish. If a State is 'reorganised' on the basis of linguistic-cultural identity, it does not mean that it belongs to a particular community.

The States were reorganised on the basis of the essence of India, which lies in its unity in diversity. A powerful institutional framework was created to govern this culturally diverse country by linking diverse regions and a democratic Government was established with 'division of powers' between the Union and culturally diverse and relatively autonomous State Governments.

If the Constitution recognises the value of cultural diversity, it also guarantees the fundamental right to every citizen, irrespective of caste, colour, creed, gender or religion, to reside in any State for pursuing trade, commerce and other professions. The Supreme Court has declared Part III of the Constitution, dealing with the Fundamental Rights of citizens, as 'the basic structure' of our democracy.

The Constitution guarantees equal rights to all citizens and Thackeray and others of his ilk cannot snatch away this right of 'North Indians' to live and work in Maharashtra. The idea of an 'outsider' comes into conflict with the idea of single citizenship. This is the reason why regional chauvinism or ethnic exclusivism has to be opposed.

Thackeray's model of politics should be opposed vigorously because if such chauvinist demands of 'localism' versus 'outsider' grow, the future of a national common market and all-India mobility will be endangered.

There are reasons to justify a tough stand against the growth of regionalism of the type that Thackeray is pursuing. First, it is unconstitutional to allow any citizen to declare another citizen as inferior on the basis of his place of birth. Second, every political party should remember that if Thackeray is not politically ostracised, he has the potential of becoming another Jarnail Singh Bhindranwale.

Bhindranwale was an ordinary Sikh preacher who wrought havoc as his anti-national activities were not nipped in the bud. Incidentally, the Congress leadership had patronised him to take on the Akali Dal.

Third, it has become a fashion to celebrate the emergence of regional parties in Indian politics and also the weakening of the all-India national parties. It has been argued that regional parties express regional aspirations; by joining coalition Governments at the Centre, they are able to reconcile regional aspirations with national interest. Is it so?

The reality of coalition Governments at the Centre, whether the NDA or the UPA, is that the regionalists have become excessively demanding. The best illustration of the fact that the balance of power has shifted from all-India parties in favour of the regionalists is provided by the policy of reservation for the OBCs. After all, the OBC quota system does not fit into the political scheme of all-India political parties.

The upshot of this narrative is that the weakening of all-India parties and the emergence of casteist, regional parties have led to a situation where national perspective has been compromised. *16 April 2008, Pioneer*

An Alliance of Opportunists: Why the UPA government is floundering

The prime ministerial system of parliamentary democracy is in a shambles because the Congress-led UPA Government does not accept the pre-eminent authority of the Prime Minister. The Prime Minister, in a parliamentary system, is not just 'one among equals'; he is the sole authoritative spokesman of his Government's domestic and foreign policies.

Unfortunately, the UPA government seems a coalition without a driver. First, Prime Minister Manmohan Singh and US President George W Bush signed a nuclear deal on July 18, 2005. But when the Prime Minister took the deal to his own coalitional partners and Parliament, it was viciously opposed both within and outside the UPA Government.

The Prime Minister, Foreign Minister and Defence Minister have been explaining to the Americans and others that the nuclear deal cannot be 'operationalised' because of political differences, especially among the coalitional partners. It is ironical that the UPA has taken three years to resolve its internal differences on the nuclear deal.

The situation has deteriorated to such an extent that the Left parties have served a notice to Singh to either bury the deal or their support to his Government will be withdrawn. Should it have taken three years to arrive at such a situation? The Prime Minister and the Congress should have held discussions on nuclear deal with the Communists and if there was no meeting ground among the coalitional partners, the deal should have been abandoned long back.

The nuclear deal should have been thrown in the waste paper basket if the Prime Minister could not convince about the merits of the deal to his own alliance partners. Generally, in a parliamentary democratic system, the ruling party has to negotiate with the Opposition to arrive at a consensus on basic national policies, especially foreign policy. The UPA, however, is writing its own story being in the Government and the Opposition at the same time.

What is the explanation for the chaotic coalitional politics of the UPA Government? First, none of the coalitional partners is ready to face the Lok Sabha election before completion of the five-year term. All coalitional partners are confined to their own region or sub-region or boundaries of a state and they have joined the UPA to maximise their gains. The caste-based regionalists have not joined the UPA to fight for national or international issues. What has M Karunanidhi to do with nuclear deal or strategic alliances? The Congress is facing political isolation because its allies are not ready to stand by the nuclear deal at the cost of losing power at the Centre.

The country's coalition politics at the Centre has highlighted the fundamental contradictions between the all-India political parties and the regional denominations. The UPA has been weakened internally by its coalition partners because there is nothing common to bind them together. 27 *June* 2008, *Pioneer*

Politics of Divorce: Ideological tripolarity will make stable alliances impossible

The Congress and the Communists had never agreed to be coalition partners because of their fundamental ideological antagonism, and the first experiment of Congress-Communist Alliance from 2004 to 2008 is coming to an end with a lot of political bitterness. While the differences between the Congress-led UPA Government and its 'outside supporters' seem to be the last straw on the camel's back, the Communists have continuously maintained that the National Common Minimum Programme agreed among the alliance partners was violated in the process of implementation of public policies during the last more than four years of the UPA Government.

It deserves to be clearly understood and emphasised that the Congress and the Left which occupy completely opposite pole of Indian politics, were never happy with the Manmohan Singh Government's policies and they had expressed their opposition many a time during the last more than four years of their 'outside association' with the UPA Government. The ideological opponents had come together to keep another ideological opponent like the BJP out of the corridors of power from 2004 to 2008.

The existing logic of 'tripolar ideological political divisions' which prevail in the country brought two ideological opponents on a common platform with the sole goal of keeping another highly committed ideological party like the BJP out of power. The purpose of this narrative is to understand clearly that the existing 'iron logic' of 'ideological tripolarity' has led and will continue to lead marriages of convenience and divorces in politics will be the order of the day. If coalition partners come together for purely 'tactical' and 'transitory' political reasons, they will also separate from one another on one pretext or the other.

Alliances among parties and groups will be formed on the basis of calculations of costs and benefits, and on the first occasion some coalition partner will walk out and some other will walk in by claiming that they are leaving or joining a coalition in defence of some principle in politics. While all regional and sub-regional groups and leaders have played politics of complete opportunism by joining or walking out of a coalition, the Congress, the BJP and the Communists, as all-India ideological political formations cannot, because of their firm ideological beliefs, play the politics of opportunism while joining or leaving coalition.

This is the context in which political divorce between the Congress and the Left has to be analysed, not only because it will leave temporary political bitterness between these two parties, this experience of 2004 to 2008 will make it difficult, even impossible, for these two ideological opponents to come together even on the basis of minimum commonly agreed programme in the future.

The Congress and the Communists are involved in a bitter ideological battle and it has already created situation where the twain shall never meet. A few facts may be mentioned to substantiate the argument that political divorce between Congress and the Left is not an ordinary reshuffling of loyalties witnessed earlier during the Janata Party experiments of VP Singh, Chandra Shekhar, HD Deve Gowda and Inder Kumar Gujaral.

Political divorce between the Congress and the Left is taking place on foreign policy and it is for the first time in the history of free India that a bitter political discourse has taken place between two alliance partners on this issue. The Congress has been completely rattled and ruffled by the Left's allegation that the Manmohan Singh Government is not following the traditional independent foreign policy; on the contrary, it is following a pro-American and subservient policy. The nuclear deal is just one illustration of this subservience.

If on the one hand, politics of principles and ideologies has become the battle ground among the three major all-India political formations, on the other, the story of an opportunist political divorce is being repeated and replayed by the Samajwadi Party represented by Mulayam Singh Yadav and Amar Singh of Uttar Pradesh. They have not only divorced the erstwhile Communist allies, but also parted company with the regional parties of the UNPA.

Clearly, politics in India is in a flux and the instability of Union Governments is bound to be inherent in such a situation. *8 July 2008, Pioneer*

Shifting Alliances: The political flux will continue till election is held

The high profile political drama of horse trading, party defection and deideologisation of parties will continue till the end of 2009 because every single political statement and action of every party, leader and group is aimed at the next Lok Sabha election. Hence, even after the Lok Sabha debate and the trust vote, political mobilisation of the voters will continue with the same hyper speed till the Lok Sabha poll.

This fact should be kept in mind while analysing the fast developing political situation in the country. A few facts may be mentioned to substantiate the argument that current hyper political activity will come to a logical end only when the Lok Sabha election is over.

First, the three main players like the Congress, the BJP and the Marxists have launched their political campaign and the withdrawal of support by the Marxists from the UPA Government on July 8, 2008 has brought these three ideological antagonists in the playground of politics and they have given a clarion call against one another. Further, these three ideological antagonists have already launched their political campaign against one another by publicly announcing their political and ideological differences.

Second, it is not only that the Congress and the Communists have decided to follow their traditional politics of confrontation and contest and by ending their marriage of inconvenience, they have begun scouting for new allies and supporters because neither the Congress nor the Communists can play any critical and crucial role without entering into alliances with regional, sub-regional parties, groups and leaders. The BJP, Like the Congress and the Communists, can play an effective role in national politics only by finding alliance partners.

Third, the history and experience of the role of allies of the Congress, the Communists and the BJP clearly show that every ally of these three major political formations has been a practitioner of real politics based on the raw logic of power for the sake of power and this history of alliances will continue to operate till the Lok Sabha election.

Fourth, the Communists after their divorce from the Congress have begun the process of forming a 'non-BJP and non-Congress' Third Front. It deserves to be clearly stated that the Communists have always failed in their effort to create a third alternative because every regional, sub-regional party, group and leader is not at all, like the Communists, burdened with the baggage of ideological commitment which keeps them together.

Communists have tried such an experiment in the past and they have not learnt any lesson from their own experience of the political fragility of the so-called Third Front. Further, political drama in Uttar Pradesh substantiates the argument that the politics of alliances is based on the calculation of quick benefits and rewards and changing allies have not hesitated to walk out or walk in from any and every alliance. Mulayam Singh Yadav of the Samajvadi party had a soft corner for the Communists and in the pursuit of his anti-Congress and anti-BJP politics had floated with great fanfare a United National Progressive Alliance with TDP, INLD, a splinter group of Assam Parishad *et al*.

But the Samajwadi Party forgot everything the moment the Left formally informed the President regarding its 'withdrawal' of outside support to the UPA – the same day, the Samajwadi Party handed over a letter of 'outside support' to the UPA Government.

The story of shifting political loyalties did not end on July 9-10. The Left then approached Ms Mayawati of the BSP to extend support against the UPA Government and she readily agreed because of the logic of Uttar Pradesh politics and not because of any ideological affirmity and new-found love for the Communists. The logic is simple: The two antagonists in Uttar Pradesh have to sail in different boats because they are major competitors in that State.

The upshot of this narrative is that politics of alliances and bargaining will dominate the scene and governance will be of secondary importance in the face of the politics of forming and breaking alliances.

Meanwhile, it needs to be clearly stated that if the Union Government has to play any role of goal oriented politics for the whole country, the political system has to be cleansed from the evil influence of unprincipled, floating MPs who are open to switching their loyalty. 22 *July* 2008, *Pioneer*

Deserting a Sinking Ship: Congress workers are sensing loss of power

The cash-for-ticket allegation leveled by senior Congress leader Margaret Alva against the leadership has more or less closed the door for her in the party, but this is not the first time that such an issue has been raised. The Congress has always fielded some rich and powerful candidates in return for 'cash' for its coffers. Hence, Ms Alva and her fellow travellers are pretenders because the practice of 'selling' tickets for fighting elections is very much in public knowledge.

It is not only for the Lok Sabha or Assembly elections that candidates who can afford the 'price' for nomination have been allowed to fight elections on a party's symbol, such practice is openly followed in the nomination of Rajya Sabha candidates where rich individuals are promised party support in return for financial gains.

Ms Alva has raised another important issue regarding the Congress's tradition of projecting progenies and children of aging leaders as natural replacements for their parents. She has stated a fact that the sons and daughters of 'important' party leaders are made automatic inheritors of the Lok Sabha constituencies or Assembly seats nourished by their parents. Ms Alva has pricked the bubble by reminding every practitioner of 'dynastic politics' in the Congress that an exception cannot be made to the rule of political inheritance followed by the party only for her son. Incidentally, Ms Alva has been herself a beneficiary of the dynastic tradition of the Congress.

Hence not only the Congress president but all big guns of the party wanted Ms Alva's blood because by raising the issue that her son was not nominated while children of many other Congress leaders were patronised, she had directly or indirectly targeted her own colleagues down the line. Yogendra Makwana, another beneficiary of the Congress, has also been served with a quit order for publicly supporting Ms Alva's allegation.

Are these and other erstwhile Congress leaders looking for political options outside the Congress family? It may also be stated that this is not the first time that Congress functionaries have either walked out or walked back into the party; nor is this the first time that the party high command has first punished them for speaking out and then brought them back. Even Mrs Indira Gandhi, who was most intolerant of any dissidence in the party, consented to restore the high position to Jagjivan Ram in 1978. He walked out of the party in 1977 when Mrs Gandhi was facing the toughest electoral challenge in her political career.

Mrs Gandhi had once publicly stated that party leaders accept her as *the leader* because she wins elections. The implication was that Congressmen tend to run away from a sinking ship. Mrs Gandhi's pubic assessment of 'loyalty' provides a key to understanding the present situation prevailing in the Congress. First, it is fully recognised by the Congress that Ms Sonia Gandhi is *the only leader* who has shown immense capacities to win elections for the party and is the architect of the Congress-led UPA coalition Government at the Centre. Party revival or winning a few elections is a necessity, but not a sufficient condition for the continuation of any leader's acceptability by a party. This is precisely what is being witnessed in the Congress.

The Congress lost the Assembly election in Karnataka, which happens to be Ms Alva's home State. It seems very plausible that she and other Congress leaders in Karnataka have been feeling politically insecure. Further, the Congress has no future not only because it has been ejected from many States, its complete marginalisation in Uttar Pradesh and Bihar has led to a situation where the party is listed in the also-ran category. In the south, Dravidian parties have successfully reduced the Congress to the status of a minor player in Tamil Nadu. In Maharashtra it cannot become a viable political force without an alliance with Sharad Pawar's NCP. The Congress is in a pathetic state in West Bengal not only because of the Communists but also because the opposition space has been taken over by Ms Mamata Banerjee.

This is precisely why its many 'loyalists' are looking for political options outside the party. The Congress is not the only route to power and when this reality sinks in, party workers start 'deserting' the sinking ship. This explains why Ms Alva and Makwana have chosen to speak out.

Also, with the rise of Rahul Gandhi as the 'nominated' successor of the Congress, the old loyalists must be feeling quite insecure and uncomfortable. This is the reason that many 'loyalists' like Arjun Singh have openly brought their sons or daughters into the mainstream of Congress politics with a view to cater to Gandhi's preference for the 'youth'. Taking a cue from this, Ms Alva not only resented the exclusion of her son from the list of party nominees, she also named Arjun Singh's son for getting nominated by the Congress for the coming Madhya Pradesh Assembly election.

The concept of 'family tree' was promoted by Mrs Indira Gandhi and thereafter has been followed by other Congress leaders who, having read the writing on the wall, are busy promoting the cause of their children. With the Congress facing declining electoral and political fortunes, we can look forward to many leaders abandoning the sinking ship and looking for greener pastures outside the Congress. *18 November 2008, Pioneer*

Parochial Politics: MNS violence can only divide society further

MNS chief Raj Thackeray's anti-north Indian campaign is clearly meant to politically weaken his uncle, Bal Thackeray's Shiv Sena. Like his uncle, he is also riding on the back of Marathi nativisim with the purpose of capturing the political space which is at present occupied by the Shiv Sena.

It is also understood that Raj Thackeray has launched the violent hate campaign with the full support, even connivance, of the Congress and NCP because any weakening of the Shiv Sena would be politically beneficial to the Congress and the NCP. The petty political games thereafter by different parties are creating a Frankenstein's monster of regional chauvinism which can lead to the weakening of the unity of India. Those sowing the seeds of violence and hatred in Maharashtra would be fully responsible for giving birth to the slow and gradual process of disintegration and balkanisation of a pluralist and diverse India.

Political developments in Maharashtra should be taken as a warning by all nationalist and patriotic forces that regional chauvinist and exclusivist assertions are a threat to the very survival of a united India. The ideological and political poison spread by Raj Thackeray has in actual practice led to a situation where taxi and three-wheeler drivers or construction workers, or other ordinary daily wage earners, have been targeted by his followers on the plea that they are 'outsiders' who have snatched jobs from the 'Marathi *manoos*'. Not only this, they have created an atmosphere of terror against north Indians.

The Railways Recruitment Board could not hold a competitive examination for the recruitment of employees in Mumbai because the 'outsiders', who have every right to participate in competitive examination held in Mumbai, were brutally assaulted by MNS workers. The Maharashtra Government did not make any arrangements for the smooth conduct of an all-India examination. And after all this, the Union Home Minister, after protests from many political leaders, reluctantly decided to talk with the State Chief Minister.

Incidentally, the President of India, the Home Minister, the Agriculture Minister, and the Aviation Minister in the Manmohan Singh Government hail from Maharashtra and none of them deemed it fit to warn the State Government that if action was not taken against the MNS chief, the unity of India would be threatened. The employment data from Maharashtra clearly shows that the Maharashtra middle and upper middle classes have an undisputed majority representation in all white collar jobs and it is only the labour class jobs that are represented by the north Indians. Has any one stopped Maharashtrian construction workers or a taxi drivers from functioning in low-paid jobs?

Regional or sub-regional identity-based politics is manipulated for political and electoral gains. Political mobilisation based on grievances – real or imaginary – is the strategy adopted by regional chauvinists and such identity-based mobilisation can succeed only on the feeling of hatred among the diverse groups in society. This is precisely the situation created by the MNS and its political collaborators in Maharashtra.

The Union Government has been always responsive to the 'sympathy' factor of the Indian Tamils in Sri Lanka and this strategy of the Government has not made Indian Tamils hostile to the Indian Government. Another laboratory of disturbed identity-based struggle is the North-East and it is worthwhile to understand the strategies followed by the Government of India to maintain national unity in the face of many secessionist campaigns in the region.

India consists of multiple regions and it has been recognised by the Constitution-makers that a democratic India can handle the problems of identity-based exclusivists and their demands can be met by the participation of all regions under a federal structure. They meant that the Union Government will have enough resources and capability to strike a balance between centrifugal and centripetal trends and tendencies. *4 November 2008, Pioneer*

Backward Politics: Mulayam has nothing to do with any school of socialism

Mulayam Singh Yadav grabbed the headlines, not for any good reason or cause when he released his party's election manifesto earlier this month because his pronouncements on 'important' issues attracted not only ridicule but also an outright hostility across intellectuals from all sections of the society.

Yadav announced that 'English cannot be a compulsory medium of communication in public life. I am not against English, but we must promote Hindi at all costs'. Just after this statement, he threw a bomb by asserting that 'English medium schools would be abolished'. Yadav's fanatically pro-Hindi and completely anti-English attitude and policy framework confine his political constituency to the backward classes and backward area of Uttar Pradesh only. He, on the basis of his stand on Hindi language, ends up as a leader of only one State out of 28 States and six Union Territories of the country. Yadav did not stop here and he further astounded the voters by announcing that the use of computers has led to the growth of unemployment. These words of wisdom place him in the category of anti-industrial revolution groups of the last decades of the 18th century Europe. Is Yadav a socialist of any kind?

Socialist thought and praxis emerged along with the development of modern industrial societies of which India is one of the latest and most important member. Modern industrialism and socialist doctrines are based on the idea of human progress, which is essentially linked with the growth of new technologies of production. Industrial Revolution was brought by scientific innovations in the field of new technologies and this was the reason that industrial societies were described as 'modern' because they had broken with the medieval feudal slave society. This narration, in brief, is essential to substantiate the argument that Yadav has nothing to do with any school of socialism.

Not only this, socialism belongs to the modern age of science and technology and Yadav is still trapped in the old belief systems of tottering mediaeval society. He literally accepted Ram Manohar Lohia's idea of backward caste peasant as a progressive social force and mobilised Yadav caste as his messengers of social change. He has nothing to do with forward-looking, change-oriented progressive ideology of socialism as he continues with his backward way of thinking and depends on his electoral victories by mobilising the support of backward caste peasants. That is precisely why he always boasted in public that he has solid support of caste-base of Yadavs and Muslims.

Especially post-Babri Mosque demolition, Yadav has exploited to the maximum the 'insecurities' of Muslims in Uttar Pradesh. This is the reason why even in 2009 he wants to placate Muslim seminary of Deoband.

Further, socialism of any variety stands for 'social equality' in society and Yadav, the so-called socialists, believes that inequality in India is caused by 'English-speaking and English-educated' social groups. Socialists in the 1950s and 1960s had launched a movement by painting English language signboard in black with a view to obliterate English symbols from the shops and roads of India. Yadav is only an inheritor of that culture. As he has been the Chief Minister of Uttar Pradesh, Yadav has a lot to answer about the total backwardness of the State in the education sector.

Why did this champion of socialism not campaigned for the universalising of elementary and primary education in his State? Apparently, Yadav does not know that the best implementation of Mid-Day Meal Scheme for school-going children is taking place not in his 'socialist' Uttar Pradesh but in Tamil Nadu. Why did the champion of the Hindi cause fail to keep Hindi-speaking States united?

The movements for the division of Uttar Pradesh are taking place because of neglect of the agenda of development. Further, had he known the elementary principles of modern economics, he would not have attributed the growing unemployment to the information technology. Yadav's thinking is local and it is impossible to expect from him any proper analysis of the causes of global recession. George Fernandes, another socialist, in 1977, had managed IBM to quit India and this one backward-looking step pushed India out of the growing technological revolution in information technology by decades.

The larger issue is regarding the failure of socialist movement in India from Lohia to Yadav. The latter is relevant in politics not because he is a believer of even elementary principles of modern progressive socialist ideology, but because he is a practitioner of casteist, and subtle communalist politics. If English were a roadblock in the progress of Uttar Pradesh then the State would have been on the top as English has already withered away in the academic universe of Yadav's sovereignty. If information technology were villain of the piece and creator of great unemployment in Uttar Pradesh, he need not worry because the State is not a candidate for any place in the field of the growth of IT industry.

The backwardness of Uttar Pradesh in every area of modernity is a product of the backward thinking parochial casteist leadership which has been at the helm of affairs. While Ms Mayawati is busy getting her statues constructed, Yadav is fighting against ghosts of modernity and progressive ideas. *29 April 2009, Pioneer*

Regionalists: Partners or spoilers

Post-Independent India had inherited the political and social umbrella platform represented by the Indian National Congress along with authentic regional political forces represented by the Akali Dal of Punjab, the National Conference (NC) of Jammu & Kashmir and the Dravdian movement and politics of Tamil Nadu. Not only this. The Communist Party and the Hindu Mahasabha had also been born in the 20th century, pre-independent India and they had contested the Lok Sabha and state assembly elections of 1952.

In other words, neither the all-India parties nor regional and sub-regional parties are new players in electoral politics. The Akali Dal, the NC and C N Annadurai's Dravida Munnetra Kazhagam have consistently opposed the centralised federal ideology of the all-India

Congress party. The Akalis, NC and DMK have, as conscious representatives of regional diversity of India, championed the cause of re-federalisation of the Constitution with a view to protect the 'autonomy' of regional cultures and interests.

The point to be understood is that a country of India's diversity and vast size requires multiple and diverse responses to specific regional and sub-regional needs and aspirations and regional parties have always been born in response to the felt needs of diverse regions.

The class architecture built by the Congress on the basis of support from high caste Hindus, Scheduled Castes and Muslims was eroded and even weakened by the emergence of powerful peasant caste groups represented by the 'Other Backward Castes' who created their own caste-based political formations. The best illustration of this is provided by the phenomenon of the emergence of caste leaders like Mulayam Singh Yadav of Uttar Pradesh and Lalu Prasad Yadav of Bihar.

These caste-based regional leaders captured political power by displacing and replacing the high-caste dominated Congress party in UP and Bihar. The peasant castes, especially OBCs of every region, felt the need to protect and promote their interests on the basis of their own political formation. However, peasant caste-based consciousness is not an all-India consciousness and this is the reason why backward caste peasantry has numerous regional parties, specifically limited to one region.

Social contradictions in agrarian society also led to the emergence of not only OBC parties but also separate parties of extremely backward castes (EBCs) and Dalits. Nitish Kumar mobilised EBCs of Bihar whose interests were in conflict with that of the Yadavs.

Ajit Singh is a leader of Jat peasants of western Uttar Pradesh who in caste hierarchy are almost equal to Yadavs but the prosperity level of Ajit Singh's Jats is higher than that of the Yadavs. Hence even among the OBCs, Ajit Singh and Mulayam Singh are not able to form one party of the backwards because intra-caste clash of interests demands a separate agenda for Jats and Yadavs.

Like the fragmented backward caste peasantry, Dalits are also fragmented. While Mayawati of the Bahujan Samaj Party has meticulously built a separate party for the Dalits of India, because of intra-Dalit conflicts, she has succeeded in establishing her supremacy only over the Dalits of Uttar Pradesh. Ram Vilas Paswan, a Dalit leader of Bihar, is not ready to accept Mayawati's claim as an unchallenged leader of Dalits outside UP. Nor are the descendants of Ambedkar in Maharashtra.

If political parties at the regional level have emerged in response to the felt needs of caste and sub-caste aspirations, the political vacuum created by the collapse of Congress in Bengal provided an opportunity to the class-based Communist parties to mobilise the urban and agrarian labouring classes, which were neglected by the Congress.

The Communist hegemony in Bengal remained unchallenged but an anti-Communist social constituency in Bengal was waiting for a leader and Mamata Banerjee emerged on the scene. The Trinamool Congress of Mamata is mobilising and leading a social constituency which remains dissatisfied with the Communist rule.

The purport of this narrative is that all regional and sub-regional parties are relevant in Indian politics because they are protecting and promoting some specific social class and group interests. The regional parties, therefore, are not a freak political phenomena. At one level, it may be suggested that Indian politics has entered a stage of regional parties versus all-India political formations.

But, at another level, it can be asserted that every major regional party is keen to participate in the exercise of power in a coalition at the central level because many regional aspirations as represented by regional parties cannot be fulfilled if they are not in power at the Centre. Thus after every Lok Sabha elections the race to form a coalition government at the Centre becomes quite hot as regional parties do not want to miss the bus.

A large number of regional parties are serious players in politics both at the level of their own state and at the Centre. Major regional parties have have enjoyed a long stint in politics as their appeal still remain relevant making them serious players in the game of politics.

13 *May* 2009, *Economic Times*

Caste no Factor: Akali domination cause of violence in Punjab

The recent violence witnessed in Punjab, a fallout of clashes between two Sikh sects at a Vienna gurdwara that led to the death of a Dera Sachkhand leader, is not only deplorable but also raises several questions over 'caste war' in that State.

It would be simplistic to explain either the recent violence or even the previous conflicts between the Dera of Guru Ravidass and the orthodox Sikh community on the basis of 'caste war' between the Dalit or Mazabi Sikhs and the upper caste practitioners of Sikhism.

It is worth recalling that just after the Akali Dal came to power in 2007, Dera Sacha Sauda chief Gurmeet Ram Rahim Singh, who faces several criminal charges, had to face violent protests tacitly supported by the Akali Dal, the Akali-controlled Sikh Gurdwara Prabhandak Committee and the Akal Takht of the Golden Temple. The Akalis got a *hukumnama* issued against Gurmeet Ram Rahim Singh by the Golden Temple.

Hence, the caste-based explanation is based on very thin evidence. The Dalit followers of Guru Ravidass being projected as targets of upper caste Sikhs is only one part of the story. The Nirankaris, another sect of the Sikh community, have been attacked many times by the followers of orthodox Sikhism. But these attacks are not on account of caste conflict.

A few facts may be mentioned to substantiate the argument that the practitioners of Sikhism-based politics want to exercise complete control over every member of the community with a view to impose their own interpretation of the doctrines of the faith.

The Akali Dal has always fought for control over the Shiromani Gurdwara Prabhandak Committee, the Golden Temple and all gurdwaras of Punjab. The Akali Dal sustains itself by drawing its authority on the basis of its control over the gurdwaras. It has always controlled dissent by getting the Akal Takht to issue *hukumnamas* against dissenters.

The Deras, which are beyond the control of the Akali Dal-controlled clergy, are thus a thorn in the flesh. Dera Sacha Sauda followers allege that their chief was attacked because they had voted for the Congress during the Assembly election in 2007.

Second, the Akali Dal consists of big farmers and prosperous entrepreneurs. This economic clout, combined with political power and theological supremacy, makes them behave as the guardians of the community. Politics of domination and resistance to any challenge to the authority of the powerful strata of the Sikh community are the causes of every conflict between the traditionalists and the Deras.

This is not the first time that the Akali Dal has actively or passively supported the assertion of Sikh dominant religious identity. The 1980s witnessed a prolonged Akali-led agitation which was later taken over by armed gangs of Bhindranwale who operated from the Golden Temple complex.

The Akalis of that era are as much responsible for the violence in Punjab during the 1980s as the Khalistanis. The Akali leadership had lost control over the movement and armed gangs, supported by foreign agencies, took over and waged war against the Indian state.

The Khalistanis were defeated but some secessionist groups have taken refuge in foreign countries and, with funds from a section of foreigners, are still pursuing the path of separatism. Pakistan still provides refuge and money to a section of the secessionists, some of whom have taken refuge in European countries. The attack on a gurdwara in Vienna has been attributed to such elements who are not happy with peace prevailing in Punjab. The Khalistani secessionists located in Europe have claimed responsibility for the attack in Vienna and the Government of India should ask frothier deportation and prosecution.

Therefore, what we recently saw in Punjab is essentially a clash between the orthodox Sikhism and those who have rejected orthodoxy. If political violence is to be controlled, a sustained ideological struggle against the monolithic interpretation of Sikhism should be launched. Otherwise Punjab will always witness sectarian violence. 2 *June* 2009, *Pioneer*

4

Foreign Policy

Samjhauta Express Blast is an attack on the ongoing confidence-building measures between India and Pakistan

The February 18 Samjhauta Express tragedy, in which 68 passengers were burnt alive while travelling from Delhi to Attari, has once again substantiated the fact that neither India nor Pakistan are immune to the threats of terrorism. This incident is a stark reminder of the post-Partition massacres, which took place in trains when innocent people were running away for life. It is estimated that one million people were the victims of the post-Partition communal frenzy.

The latest tragedy is a reminder of the fact that the Partition could not completely separate the migrants to India and Pakistan from their respective native places. The decision to start the Samjhauta Express has been dictated by the existing reality of human problems of 'divided' families in the two countries. The terrorists cannot accept the normalisation of relations between India and Pakistan, even though such a move would benefit the common man of the two countries the most.

The end of hostilities between India and Pakistan will not only be beneficial to the industrial and trading classes but also the separated families of the lower middle class. It deserves to be clearly stated that the real people to people peace constituency consists of 'separated' families which are longing to visit India or Pakistan to meet their relatives.

The first and foremost lesson from the Black Sunday is that India and Pakistan should continue to make efforts to strengthen mutual relations. It is heartening to note that Pakistan's Foreign

Minister Khurshid Mahmud Kasuri not only went ahead with his official journey to India, but he also stated, 'Incidents like these, which are heart-rending and which affect both countries, can only add to the urgency for the need for cooperation'. It has been recognised by India and Pakistan that the terrorist attack on the Samjhauta Express on the eve of the official meeting of the Foreign Ministers of the two countries has a diabolical intention of derailing the ongoing peace process.

It is for the first time that the Government of India has not blamed Pakistan-trained terrorist outfits for the Samjhauta Express blast. The mainstream media in both the countries, too, did not indulge in the exercise of accusations.

In hindsight, it can be stated that Prime Minister Manmohan Singh and General Pervez Musharraf were sagacious enough to establish a joint-mechanism on terrorism and at the 2006 Havana Conference of non-aligned nations, both the leaders regarded terrorism as a double-edged weapon that requires joint tackling. It is, therefore, surprising that an idea of a 'joint probe', as suggested by Pakistan's National Assembly, has been dismissed by the Government of India. It was a good opportunity for the two countries to work together.

There was no harm if India had agreed to the idea of a 'joint probe', as suggested by Pakistan. It is good that information gathered by India will be shared with Pakistan at an anti-terrorist joint mechanism meeting on March 6. A socially disturbed and weakened Pakistan has the potential to be a great headache to India and it is essential that 'composite dialogue' and 'confidence-building measures' between these two countries is accelerated.

It is suggested that like the India-Pakistan Joint Anti-Terrorism Mechanism, a joint group on Jammu & Kashmir, too, should be set up. The UPA Government has the necessary political support to pursue the resolution of bilateral disputes with Pakistan.

Gen Musharraf has been working under more constraints than Manmohan Singh because in Pakistan, a powerful section of the Army and fanatic religious groups have a vested interest in pursuing rabid anti-India policies. Unlike Pakistan, India can politically manage its fanatic anti-Pakistan lobby better because mainstream India is interested in finding solutions to the 60-year-old dispute.

The beginning of the 21st century has completely changed the context of the India-Pakistan relationship. India and Pakistan cannot afford to be adventurist any more because the military powers will not allow any misadventure on the part of the two nuclear powers in South Asia. In this changed scenario, it is impossible for the two countries to resolve their bilateral disputes by fighting wars. Negotiated answers to the Jammu & Kashmir issue must be found.

Neither India nor Pakistan can impose its will on the resolution of the Jammu & Kashmir issue. The path of terrorism is dangerous because terrorist outfits cannot succeed in imposing any political solution on India. Moreover, anyone in India or Pakistan who believes in the efficiency of subversive methods, should know that terrorism is counter-productive. The choice for India and Pakistan is to live with a 'disturbed' Jammu & Kashmir or find solutions which are reasonable and acceptable to both the countries.

The Line of Control has to be symbolically accepted by India and Pakistan and Jammu & Kashmir is to be governed by autonomous local Governments under the overall protective umbrella of joint control by India and Pakistan. A lesson can be learnt from the India-Bhutan relationship.

A military solution to the issue of Jammu & Kashmir is not available in this nuclear era. The ongoing terrorist activities in India and Pakistan, too, have failed to achieve anything. The bleeding of the people of Jammu & Kashmir can come to an end only by arriving at a negotiated settlement of this 'dispute' between the two countries. The status quo should not continue because the continuation of the stalemate is not beneficial to either country.

The upshot of the above explanation is that the Samjhauta Express blast is an attack on the ongoing confidence-building measures between India and Pakistan. When the armies have failed, terrorists cannot succeed in changing the boundaries of countries or destroying the will of states to manage their affairs. The only achievement of terrorism is to make states ruthless and militarised. Peace has to be negotiated and terrorists have to be made irrelevant in finding any long-term solution to the Jammu & Kashmir issue. *28 February 2007, Pioneer*

Trust Deficit in SAARC: The Delhi Summit highlighted differences between member-states

India's foreign policy cannot move forward without the resolution of its disputes with Pakistan and China. This situation of 'neighbourly' distrust cannot be changed without overcoming the historical memories of the Jammu & Kashmir issue between India and Pakistan and China's ambitions of becoming an Asian superpower. The 14th SAARC summit has once again substantiated the fact that India, Pakistan and China are pulling in different directions. This is the reason why, unlike other regional associations, SAARC has always been engaged in discussing peripheral issues, leaving contentious ones for bilateral discussions.

The eight-member SAARC summit ended without any fireworks or public display of inter-regional hostilities. This became possible because India and Pakistan have reached a conclusion that bilateral disputes can only be settled by long and rigorous negotiations. The two countries have realised that any war, conventional or otherwise, for conflict-resolution is no longer an option after the nuclearisation of the subcontinent.

The New Delhi summit was held when every member-state is not only engaged in combating cross-border terrorism, but also facing challenges from domestic practitioners of violence. India is grappling with violence practised by Maoists, Sri Lanka is facing an ethnic civil war and Gen Pervez Musharraf of Pakistan is riding dangerously on the back of Islamic fundamentalists. President Hamid Karzai of Afghanistan is fighting a bitter war against Pakistan-based and indigenous Taliban groups. As far as Bangladesh is concerned, it has often been accused of being soft on Islamist terrorists, inimical to India's interests.

South Asia is trying to grapple with the changed scenario of the 21st century. One aspect of the new reality was witnessed at the Delhi SAARC summit, in which China, Japan, South Korea, the European Union and the United States were invited as 'observers'. The very fact the Russia was absent from the summit is a clear evidence of the fact that a new global order has emerged after the collapse of erstwhile Soviet Union.

The end of the Cold War has led to the emergence of the US-led unipolar world order. This new reality has impacted every country of the world and without exception, SAARC is keen to 'integrate' its economies and strategic doctrines with the sole superpower.

The Karzai Government in Afghanistan and the military dictatorship of Gen Musharraf will collapse like a house of cards without the US's assistance. India has abandoned its traditional foreign policy of non-alignment and is negotiating with the US on the issue of nuclear energy. Without America's sanction, the Nuclear Suppliers Group will not cooperate with any country on the issue of nuclear energy. No wonder India, as a leading member of SAARC, has welcomed the US as an 'observer' for the summit.

Every country in the South Asian region is standing in a queue to integrate itself with the US. In contrast, the South Asian Free Trade Agreement (SAFTA) has been facing difficulties in its implementation. This fact has been testified by a World Bank Study of 2007 on 'South Asia Growth and Regional Integration'. This World Bank report says that inter-regional and intra-regional trade promotion has many hurdles to cross before SAFTA can become an integrative force.

The Annual Report of the Ministry of Defence Affairs, 2006-07, says, 'India is continuing to have security concerns with Pakistan on cross-border terrorism. Terrorist groups continue to operate freely in Pakistan. They also find shelter, support and training for operations across the LoC from elements in Pakistan'. India's worries about Pakistan do not end with the problem of cross-border terrorism.

The Annual Report adds, 'The Chinese assistance to Pakistan's nuclear and missile programmes has been a matter of concern as it has adversely impacted on India's national security environment. India keeps an eye on China's help to Pakistan's nuclear plan'. So, the fact of the matter is that India, Pakistan, Bangladesh and China are all facing a mutual 'confidence deficit' which can only be overcome by sustained negotiations.

It is too simplistic to suggest that growing economic interdependence in the region facilitates the emergence of good neighbourly relations. After all, politics, and not economics, alone can break barriers of mutual discord. Unlike the EU, SAARC was formed amid clouds of suspicion, hostility and fear. Its latest summit has clearly shown that a low level of confidence exists among the member-states which have to cross many hurdles before ushering in normalcy in the region. *10 April 2007, Pioneer*

Caution Warranted

India has many stories and multiple historical narratives continue to play a decisive role in the shaping of our attitude towards family, marriage and other levels of socio-cultural interactions. A village *biradari* takes a collective decision on issues of marriage. Not only are the dos and don'ts of marriages decided but also slight violations are punished by the *biradari*. The greatest affront to the *biradari*-imposed norms is inter-caste or inter-religious marriages. The *biradari* hunts such violators and severe punishment, including death, is imposed on the 'rebels'. Elopement is unacceptable to the 'custodians' of Indian tradition.

An important ingredient of Indian arranged marriages is the horoscopes of the prospective couple. Here, the extended family and priests play a significant role in decision-making. It was quite starkly evident recently when the Bachchan family made Aishwarya Rai marry with a 'tree' to get rid of the evil influences of her 'defective' stars and planets. Ironically, if this is the case with a 'love' marriage, one wonders what will happen in arranged ones. This is the best example of the worst kind of superstition-based tradition followed by a family which claims to be 'modern', be it arranged or love marriage?

It is quite legitimate that parents would be concerned about the welfare of their children and their involvement in an important decision like marriage. Parental anxiety is always reflected when negotiations for marriage of their children are underway. The problem arises when parental anxiety becomes so excessive that it ends up in forcing a decision on reluctant children. Concern for the future happiness and security of married couple should not become an obsession where the likes and dislikes of children are completely ignored.

Adolescent children have to be taken care of by parents because they have many questions and are unable to find proper answers. Parental guidance during adolescence is part of proper education and it is the absence of such parental guidance that non-adult children decide to do things which they may repent later. Marriage is a relationship that merits a mature decision as two 'unknown' adults are tying the knot and every couple faces problems of adjustment, whether marriage is arranged or based on love. And this is the root cause of problems.

Many love marriages have ended in nasty divorces. Arranged marriages with full blessings and consent of parents may lead to happiness or grief. An effort has to be made to arrive at a balance between the wisdom and experience of the parents and the likes and dislikes of the future bride and bridegroom. That marriages are made in heaven and destiny is determined by 'stars' have become clich?d.

Children must develop a level of confidence in themselves and their parents on issues like marriage. Elopement stories are based on trust deficit within the family. Many a time parents impose their decisions on reluctant children and a situation develops when they are forced to run away. The stories of elopement must make parents and extended family to sit together and identify the reasons for distrust which exists between children and the elders.

The period of adolescence is tricky and parental guidance as friends and philosophers is an imperative input for the healthy emotional growth of a child. Social conservatism and liberal modern attitudes towards children are myths. Parental love is a balancing factor in the life of a child.

The upshot of the above narration is that the family has to play a crucial role in the upbringing of children, though I accept that even this does not assure a happy marriage. Parental anxiety about the future of their married children is a part of the natural component of culturally determined personalities of Indians. But the 'gen-next' needs to be treated differently, thanks to shrinking of the world and the Western culture reaching the bedrooms of Indian middle-class families.

As a grandfather, it will give me great pain if my dearest ones commit blunder in selecting their partner. I will assist, advice and guide them. It is my duty and responsibility. *22 April 2007, Pioneer*

We don't Need to Cross Oceans When Options of Strategic Alliance are Available in Asia, with Russia and China

The UPA Government has, for wrong reasons, put all its eggs in the American basket. The process of the ongoing negotiations between India and the US on the 123 Agreement reveals that India is a supplicant and an applicant for nuclear deal with Americans.

Henry Sokolski, head of the Non-Proliferation Policy Education Centre, stated in the *USA Today* on April 13, 'The Indians are being greedy'. According to Sokolski, India wants to keep its options open for future nuclear testing, but it is not acceptable because the American law does not permit an ally to undertake nuclear tests. Then, Foreign Secretary Shiv Shankar Menon had to rush to the US to sort out the bottlenecks.

US Undersecretary of State Nicholas Burns, too, stated on April 13 that the three rounds of talks on the 123 Agreement have shown little results. He said, 'I don't question India's goodwill, but there is a fair degree of frustration in Washington that the Indian Government has not engaged seriously enough or quickly enough with both the US and the IAEA'.

Ironically, the Government has failed to shown any strength to reject the American conditionalities on the nuclear deal. It deserves to be stated that the Manmohan Singh Government's engagement with the US cannot be understood by focusing attention on the nuclear deal alone. Burns observed on April 30, 'Within a generation Americans may view India as one of our two or three most important strategic partners'.

It is both unnecessary and dangerous for Indian foreign policy-makers to operate in the context of the US-led unipolar system. A developing country like India will be benefited if the international system operates on the basis of checks and balances and it is possible only if the existing American unilateralism is replaced by effective multiple centres of power.

It is wrong on the part of Indians to accept that they are destined to live under the shadow of American hegemony because new possibilities for the birth of multiple centres of power are emerging. Russian President Vladimir Putin attracted global attention to American hegemonic designs in Munich. He reiterated his opposition to the emergence of hegemonic world order on April 26 in his Annual State of the Nation Address in which he accused the US-led NATO countries for strengthening their 'military presence in Eastern Europe' with a view to encircle Russia.

Appropriate lessons should be drawn from the growing rift between Russia and the US. Russia ratified the Conventional Armed Forces Treaty in Europe, leading to the liquidation of the Warsaw Pact. The US, in contrast, has not only refused to ratify the CFE treaty, but also is engaged in expanding the reach of NATO countries.

Such a breach of trust has led Putin to observe on April 26, 'Refusing to ratify the CFE treaty under far-fetched pretexts they are using this situation to expand a network of military bases near our borders. Moreover, they are planning to deploy components of a missile defence system in the Czech Republic and Poland... I think it will be expedient to declare a moratorium on Russian Compliance with the (CFE) treaty until all NATO member countries ratify it'.

The West is deeply engaged in funding the 'pro-democracy'

organisations in the erstwhile republics of the Soviet Union with a view to have compliant crony states in the region. India, like Russia, has great stakes in Central Asia for energy resources. India, therefore, needs a close collaboration with Russia for safeguarding its energy interests in the region. Moreover, we must not forget that the 21st century is going to be Asia's century.

Russia, along with Central Asian countries, is a formidable economic and strategic power in this part of the world and India cannot bypass the logic of regional geography. China, too, has love-hate relations with the US. Our foreign policy-makers have a great opportunity to establish friendly relations with Russia and China not only for mutual benefits, but also with a view to establish a 'countervailing force' against American hegemony.

Unfortunately, our policy-makers are not ready to draw any lessons from the experiences of Russia and China. India must realise that the US is following a foreign policy of interventionism in the domestic affairs of other countries in the name of democracy and human rights. Its attempt to interfere in the Indo-Iranian relationship only proves the point.

The US's foreign policy adventurism needs to be checked by the collective efforts of India, Russia and China. This arrangement is more beneficial to India than the idea of being a so-called strategic ally of the US. We don't need to cross oceans when options are available in the mainland of Asia. *7 May 2007, Pioneer*

Message from Lal Masjid: Religion must be kept at an arm's length from the affairs of state

The chickens have come home to roost for the Pakistani state, which has patronised fanatic religious groups to pursue pernicious policies of destabilising its neighbours like India and Afghanistan. It was a day of reckoning for President Pervez Musharraf when he ordered the Army to liquidate the *jihadis* holed up in Lal Masjid.

A few facts may be mentioned to understand the context that led Gen Musharraf to take on the Islamists. Ayesha Jalal, the author of *Jinnah: The Sole Spokesman*, has described Pakistan as a formal Islamic state. She, however, has missed the point that 'formal Islamic state' may end up becoming a theocratic state.

Not just Pakistan, any religion-based state would become an instrument at the hands of religious puritans because a religion based on a book is dependent upon its different interpretations by competing schools of thought. Christianity is replete with examples where people have been declared infidels and ex-communicated for their conflicting interpretation of the Bible.

Moreover, all dictators of Pakistan – from Ayub Khan to Gen Musharraf – have actively aided in making that country's society extremist. The recent Army intervention in the Lal Masjid imbroglio is nothing but the epitomisation of clash between Islamic fundamentalism and the state.

It was the 1979 US-USSR standoff in Afghanistan that resulted in the formation of groups like the Taliban. The US patronised and mobilised *jihadis* to fight against the erstwhile Soviet Union. Pakistan actively supported the US in its fight against Soviet forces. In the process, the successive Governments of Pakistan became a pawn of the larger American gameplan. So, the seeds of religious extremism were sown in 1979. However, the American contribution towards Islamisation of Muslim societies has not been limited only to Afghanistan and Pakistan.

In its fight against terrorism, the US has found Gen Musharraf as a trustworthy ally. Thus, Pakistani society, which had already been distorted by the presence of armed religious groups, provided a solid institutionalised support to Islamist terrorists.

The US and China have been close friends of Pakistan for decades, but the Islamists have started targeting even their citizens in Pakistan. So, Gen Musharraf was under great pressure from both these countries to act against the *jihadis* holed up in Lal Masjid. Islamist terrorists have no concern for the nationality of their opponents. They would kill anyone whom they consider to be threatening their religion.

Finally, the Pakistani regime believed that by propping up

religious fundamentalists against India in Jammu & Kashmir, they would snatch it away from India. But Pakistan's misadventure against India has not brought any dividends. Since 9/11, global opinion on Islamist terrorism has become quite hostile and Americans have pressurised Gen Musharraf to curb their activities.

As the analysis suggests, Gen Musharraf had been cornered and as a last resort, he asked the Army to get Lal Masjid vacated and also convey a message that he is still in total command. Incidentally, the military operation in Lal Masjid can be compared with the Blue Star Operation of June 5, 1984, when Jarnail Singh Bhindranwale-led religious fanatics had to be evacuated from Golden Temple of Amritsar.

The first lesson from the Lal Masjid experience is that religion has to be kept away from the corridors of power. Second, it is simplistic to maintain that state can manipulate religious groups and abandon them after its objective is achieved. A secular state apparatus is not possible if religious fanatics are legitimised by the powers-that-be.

A section of the Pakistani Army is infected by religious extremism and terrorist attacks on Gen Musharraf cannot take place without its connivance.

It's clear that patronising of religious groups by state functionaries for political purposes in South Asia has played havoc. Indeed, a flawed democracy is better than a dictatorship because religion-based parties get marginalised in a competitive democratic electoral system. This is the message from Lal Masjid. *17 July 2007, Pioneer*

Military Dictatorship in India's Western Neighbourhood has Feudal Roots

The people of Pakistan have once again lost their freedom because President Pervez Musharraf, by proclaiming an Emergency on November 3, has established a completely undemocratic regime. Gen Musharraf defended his move on the basis of an alibi that 'the country's determined fight against extremists and terrorists groups has been obstructed by judicial pronouncements and judgements dealing with terrorist and anti-national violent groups'.

Incidentally, it is not the first time that the Pakistani people have been denied their basic human right to govern their country on the basis of their democratically elected representatives. It is a worrisome situation for India as well because a completely militarised and nuclearised country under the control of a dictator can take irresponsible action towards its neighbour.

The latest political developments in Pakistan should make us ponder about the causes which have obstructed development of democratic forces in that country for the past 60 years. There is also a need to compare the contrasting experience of India, the world's largest democracy. Why are these neighbouring countries following completely opposite political systems in spite of the fact that they took birth on the same day – August 15, 1947?

Many facile arguments have been given to substantiate the argument that unlike India, Pakistan's formative years were politically interrupted by the death of Mohammed Ali Jinnah and the assassination of Liaquat Ali Khan. It has been suggested that democracy in newly liberated countries deserves to be nurtured by sagacious leaders. Pakistan, therefore, was unfortunate on this count.

In India, however, the Congress, under the leadership of Jawaharlal Nehru, played the role of striking the roots of democracy between 1947 and 1964. Pakistan was deprived of this asset because both Jinnah and Khan could not live long to guide the nation. The logic still does not explain the *coup d'etat* of Gen Ayub Khan and the end of democracy in Pakistan.

Pakistan missed another chance when Zulfiquar Ali Bhutto, after the dismemberment of Pakistan and with complete delegitimisation of the Pakistan Army, failed to write a new chapter on the India-Pakistan relationship. Why did Bhutto fail to establish democracy in Pakistan? He was soon overthrown by Gen Zia-ul-Haq. The same story was repeated in the late 1980s and the 1990s. This time the political players were elected Prime Ministers – Ms Benazir Bhutto and Nawaz Sharif – and the man-in-uniform was Gen Pervez Musharraf, who imposed military dictatorship in October 1999.

It is simplistic to suggest that people had lost faith in their democratically elected leaders and allowed military dictatorships to rule over Pakistan. The explanation for India and Pakistan following different political systems lies in the social structures of the two countries. After all, society and politics are linked with one another because politics of any country does not hang in the air and is always linked with society.

First, India and Pakistan followed different paths in dealing with exploitative feudal and landlord agrarian systems. Democracy based on the principles of liberty and equality cannot operate in feudal set-up. David Ricardo, a well-known founder of political economy, wrote in his *Principles* in 1815: 'Landlord class is the enemy of all other classes'. He was referring to the new class of industrialists, entrepreneurs, professionals and working classes in industrialising England of the 19th century. Feudalism operates on the basis of slavery, suppression and oppression; and, it is only by establishing a complete and unlimited control over the majority of working population. India after independence abolished 560 princely states, the citadels of feudalism, and passed land reforms laws for the abolition of landlords. Pakistan, on the other hand, failed to abolish feudalism.

Second, Pakistan's Army officers were integrally linked with their feudal and landlord families. Pakistan's Army officials are not only the usurper of political power, but also important economic actors in that country. If the Indian Army is a professional middle class, then the Pakistan Army is a ruling class and its Generals are big economic players in Pakistani society.

Third, the Pakistani ruling classes, consisting of powerful landlords, industrialists and civil service officials along with extremely rich and prosperous political leaders, have collectively decided to hand over their country to the Americans whether during the 40 years of the Cold War era or during the US's war against terrorism. The Army in Pakistan is not only in commanding position in its society, economy and polity, it is also treated as a 'special extension' of the US.

The upshot of the above narrative is that democracy in Pakistan can have safe passage only if the base of economic power of landlords and Army is destroyed. Otherwise, social authoritarianism will continue to sustain political dictatorship. *30 November 2007, Pioneer*

The Debate in Parliament on the 123 Agreement has Achieved Nothing

The Lok Sabha has clinically scrutinised the pros and cons of the India-US nuclear deal and it is possible that the UPA Government may conclude that the members of the Lower House have endorsed the 123 Agreement at the end of a lively debate on November 28. However, it deserves to be stated that the House in general is not in favour of the nuclear deal.

The Government stands completely isolated from the mainstream Opposition parties. The debate of November 28 has revealed that the Government is following foreign policy which is quite unpopular with the people of India, as shown by the stand taken by the Opposition parties in the Lok Sabha.

The three major political parties – the Congress, the BJP and the CPI(M) – have taken positions on the floor of the House which deserve to be highlighted to substantiate the argument that the UPA does not represent majority public opinion on its foreign policy. The Government's stand is a parrot like repeat performance of the past than two to three years by US President George W Bush and Prime Minister Manmohan Singh.

The Government has not put forward any new argument on November 28. The India-US cooperation, according to the UPA Government, is a 'passport' for the country to travel to the world to 'conduct nuclear trade'. The 123 Agreement, in reality, lays down 'conditionalities' on India and the Government is not ready to face this reality.

Leader of Opposition LK Advani has stated in the Lok Sabha:

'The 123 Agreement, as it stands today, is unacceptable... No self-respecting country can agree to it. There is no flip-flop by us and we are not anti-American in our approach like the Left'. He also warned that 'if they (BJP) came to power, it would 'negotiate' the deal, and if it fails, the BJP would reject it'.

The bone of contention between the UPA Government and the BJP is that the post-nuclear deal phase will lead to the erosion of India's sovereignty to 'test nuclear bomb on the basis of our security threat perceptions'. The BJP has not bought a verbal assurance of the Government that after the IAEA agreement and the conclusion of negotiations with the Nuclear Suppliers' Group, India will have the sovereign 'option' to conduct 'nuclear test' if it is in national interest.

The Left parties have been consistently opposing the foreign and strategic foreign polices of the UPA Government because they have maintained that the Manmohan Singh regime 'has completely deviated from India's traditional foreign policy of national independence and anon-alignment'. The Communists maintain that India has distanced itself from its traditional allies like Iran at the behest of the US.

It is not relevant to suggest that the Communists are ideologically conditioned to oppose the US and on the basis of this ideological package, they want India to maintain safe distance from that country. Is it non-empirical to be cautious of the US's global designs? Is it being doctrinaire to ignore the US's track record of interventionism in the internal affairs of other countries? Do we need an anti-American ideology to evaluate the carrot-and-stick policies of sole superpower?

Trade alone is not a motive force for the Bush Administration. The CPI(M) stated in the Lok Sabha, 'The Americans need India to maintain a balance of power in South and South-East Asia. They are getting isolated in the world due to their policies. Is it in our interest if we be a party to it?' The US's National Security Strategy, 2002, has observed that India and China are 'potential US rivals' and in 2007, it is fruitful for the Americans to win over India as an ally.

Manmohan Singh should have launched discussions on the nuclear deal with the BJP and the Communists just after signing the July 18, 2005 India-US nuclear declaration. The UPA is quite concerned about the erosion of India's international credibility if the nuclear deal is rejected. The Government has to blame itself for creating a situation where it finds itself politically isolated because it had not considered it appropriate to resolve political differences with the opponents of the nuclear deal.

The upshot of above narrative is that the Lok Sabha debate has not helped the Government to get political 'endorsement' of the India-US nuclear deal and the blame lies squarely with the Government. After all, on such a crucial national policy, it adopted either the postures of arrogance or of holding selective discussions with selected groups. The India-US nuclear deal is a national issue and the Government completely failed to realise its national importance; else, it would have held broad-based national discussions with major political parties. *11 December 2007, Pioneer*

Lessons from China Visit: UPA's Beijing policy is better than its Washington policy

The UPA Government has pursued a foreign policy which has been opposed by some major political parties, groups and leaders. The Government, however, has something to cheer about: Prime Minister Manmohan Singh's three-day visit to China has received a positive response from BJP leader LK Advani and the Communists. The BJP's support to the Congress-led Government's foreign policy on China is a positive development because ticklish issues of bilateral relations between the two neighbours cannot be resolved without national consensus.

The India-China relations have never been smooth, especially after the 1962 war. This political deadlock was further crystallised by China's support to Pakistan in 1965 and 1971. China's pro-Pakistan foreign and defence policies were interpreted negatively by our policy-makers. A little step forward was taken by Rajiv Gandhi during his visit to China in 1988. The BJP-led NDA Government further opened 'dialogue' with China. No wonder a policy framework between the two nations was reached in April 2005.

The main feature of Manmohan Singh's visit to China was the signing of a statement which said: 'A shared vision for the 21st century' will guide the two neighbours who will work as 'partners, not rivals'. A proposal for 'high quality' Regional Trading Agreement has been made. On the contentious boundary issue, the two Prime Ministers – Manmohan Singh and Wen Jiabao – stated that it would be 'boundary of peace and friendship'. Further, the 'two sides hold that the right of each country to choose its own path of social, economic and political development in which fundamental human nights and the rule of law are given their due place, should be respected'. It could be stated that a positive framework of co-existence between India and China has emerged during this visit.

The UPA Government must learn lessons that foreign policy based on serious domestic political cleavages cannot succeed because a politically divided nation cannot get global acceptance. External Affairs Minister Pranab Mukherjee had to eat an humble pie when he publicly admitted on January 11, while dealing with the India-US nuclear deal: 'We have to carry out supporters with us because if they (the Left parties) withdraw support, then the Government will be in a minority. Nobody is going to sign an international agreement of this nature with a minority Government'.

The Congress should not blame anyone except itself for its Government's foreign policy debacle on the nuclear deal, as it failed to reach any domestic consensus on the issue.

The Congress has failed to understand the logic of numbers in parliamentary democracy and is caught in a fix because the Communists cannot allow any 'pro-America foreign policy' to be pursued by the UPA. The Left parties are not wrong because it is not just the question of the nuclear deal. The Manmohan Singh Government has also announced India's 'Strategic Partnership' with the US. It is well-known that any 'partnership' with the US means supporting its aggressive foreign policy, too.

The proclaimed foreign policy of the US is to safeguard its oil, energy and strategic interests across the world. India will have to be either passive or neutral in these global conflicts created by the Americans. Moreover, the US is known for interfering in the domestic affairs of sovereign countries and following a policy of 'hot pursuit' against 'terrorists' in other nations. Is this policy of direct interference acceptable to India? India and China have stated on January 14 that every country has a right to 'choose its own path'. This foreign policy approach is contradicted by the US's assertions of 'hot' pursuit of terrorists wherever they are alleged to be operating.

The UPA Government has broken national consensus on foreign policy by unilaterally deciding to agree to terms and conditions of the Americans on the nuclear deal. It is a clear reflection on the cavalier way the Manmohan Singh Govern-ment has treated Indian public opinion. The worst part of the story is that the UPA Government does not accept the fact that it has failed to sell the nuclear deal to the people.

The upshot of the above narrative is that while the Manmohan Singh Govern-ment has got well-deserved brickbats for its pro-US foreign policy, it has earned support across party lines for its China policy. The UPA Government must learn from the two experiences.
22 January 2008, Pioneer

The PPP-PML(N) Government is a Temporary Marriage of Convenience as the Two Parties Represent Different Social Constituencies

Pakistan witnessed a free, fair and competitive election on February 18 and the old warhorses represented by the Pakistan People's Party and the Pakistan Muslim League (Nawaz) emerged powerful enough to form a coalition Government at the Centre. On March 25, a nominee of the PPP, Syed Yusuf Raza Gillani, was sworn in as Prime Minister of Pakistan.

There is little doubt that the PPP-PML(N) coalition seems to be a temporary marriage of convenience because Nawaz Sharif has decided to support the PPP Government from 'outside'. On March 25, Sharif observed: ' Zardari kept insisting and we finally accepted. This is a bitter medicine we had to swallow. For the bigger cause of reinstating the deposed judges, we have scarified'.

The assassinated PPP leader, Benazir Bhutto, and Sharif had fought bitter political battles against each other. Asif Ali Zardari, the PPP co-chairman, should be prepared for opposition from Sharif because the PPP and the PML(N) represent different social class and region-based social constituencies. So, contradictions among different social constituencies represented by these two parties are bound to emerge in future.

Sharif and Zardari will have to grapple with the problem of terrorist violence in Pakistan. Moreover, the US is not likely to leave the 'war on terror' to the Government of Pakistan. Incidentally, Bhutto had come to Pakistan from her exile by making commitments to the US Administra-tion to continue a 'joint struggle' against terrorism in Pakistan. The day Gillani assumed the office of Prime Minister, the two high-ranking American functionaries – US Deputy Secretary of State John Negroponte and Assistant Secretary of State Richard Boucher – landed in Pakistan to engage the new Government in its 'war on terror'.

According to the US Administration, an ally is needed to target terrorists in Pakistan who are hurting American interests in Afghanistan. Petroleum supply from Pakistan to Afghanistan is targeted by Pakistan-based terrorists and it affects the US's war on terror. It deserves to be stated that the US is not concerned if Pakistani-based terrorists indulge in violence against India, but attacks against Afghanistan are not acceptable to it.

Sharif in his meeting with US State Department functionaries said: 'The Basic issue is that as the US wants to be safe from terrorism, we don't want to see bombs and missiles falling on our villages, we want our people to be safe and we don't want blood to flow'. This means he does not agree with the US policy of 'hot pursuit' of terrorists in Pakistan's frontier areas – a policy which the Americans were following during Gen Pervez Musharraf's dictatorship. It is an important political position taken by Sharif on the issue of war on terror. His stance is not only in contradiction with the American strategy on terror, but will also create problems between Sharif and Zardari, thanks to Bhutto's 'commitments' to the US before her arrival in Pakistan.

Terrorism in Pakistan has come to stay and its political leadership will have to arrive at an understanding with Army Generals on their role in fighting terror under the guidance of a democratic Government. There is no evidence that the Army has accepted the authority of the civilian Government in Pakistan. However, democracy in Pakistan is not under threat from the Army alone; it is also under siege because fundamentalist organisations and institutions wish to capture the state apparatus with the help of bullet and not of ballot.

Today, Pakistan is confronted with a deadly cocktail of religious fundamentalism and gun-wielding terrorists. A contradiction seems to be emerging between the approaches of the US and Sharif on how to fight terrorism in Pakistan and it is not without reason that the Bush Administration has showcased its clout to the new Government by announcing a grant of $ 300 million on March 27.

It deserves to be stated that the PPP and the PML(N) were at the helm of affairs in the pre-Musharraf era and had encouraged radical Islamism in that country. It seems unlikely that they have learnt any lesson from their mistakes. Terrorism in Pakistan is a product of domestic religio-political forces supported and was financed by the US during its war against the USSR in Afghanistan for a decade since 1979.

Pakistan has often been betrayed by its elected leaders. One hopes history doesn't repeat itself and Islamabad gets out of the Army-*mullah* nexus to witness a flourishing democracy. This is good not just for that country but also the world. *1 April 2008, Pioneer*

UPA's American Dream: India has never been so divided on foreign policy

On April 23, External Affairs Minister Pranab Mukherjee assured the country that the proposed India-US nuclear deal will soon be placed before Parliament for full discussion. Mukherjee said, 'Before we go for its ratification in the American Congress, we will come to Parliament to take the sense of the House even though there is no provision in the Constitution that stands in our way'.

Mukherjee's statement reveals his incapacity to pilot the nuclear deal because of political opposition in the country. The Congress leadership has to be blamed for its failure to carry conviction with major political parties about the correctness of its foreign policy. It is for the first time since independence that the Congress leadership has divided the country on foreign policy. After all, India's foreign policy between 1947 and 2004 was based on national consensus.

A few facts may be mentioned to substantiate the argument that the Congress-led UPA Government will go out of office with a baggage of failed foreign policy initiatives. The Congress leadership has been proved bankrupt for its failure to understand the public and political mood within the country, especially while dealing with the US. The Communists have consistently stated that they will 'withdraw their outside support' to the UPA Government if India's sovereignty was 'mortgaged' to the Americans. The BJP, with the strength of 138 Lok Sabha MPs, too, has distanced itself from the UPA Government's proposed nuclear deal. The BJP has an apprehension that by supporting the India-US nuclear deal, Indians will lose their sovereign right to conduct nuclear test in future.

Why does the Congress continue with the pro-American policy despite such public and political opposition? The Congress's non-responsive attitude towards its political allies and opponents cannot be attributed to its arrogance of power or because of its lack of experience to manage a coalition Government. The explanation has to be culled from the inside story of the present Congress leadership. A section of Congress leadership is neither interested nor does it understand the changing complexities of global situation in the 21st century. This section represents courtiers and sycophants who wield power within the Congress by repeatedly proclaiming their loyalty to the Nehru-Gandhi family. Another section within the present Congress leadership is ideologically committed to the policy of integration of Indian economy, polity and society with the advanced centres of capitalism. This group looks towards the US for economic development and strategic security alliances for India. It is because of these two groups that is shaping the UPA's foreign policy.

The above narrative suggests that the Congress has an active group within the party that looks towards the US for the protection and promotion of India's national interests. Ironically, this group is supported by Congress president Sonia Gandhi. Unfortunately for the Congress, the country thinks differently and it is because of public mood that Mukherjee had to reluctantly come out with a public statement on April 22 that 'Iran's nuclear programme is subject to verification by the IAEA' alone, and not by any other country.

It is well known that the US has been interfering in India's foreign affairs, particularly its policy towards Iran. The proposal for a gas pipeline from Iran to India via Pakistan did not find favour with the Americans and they had publicly asked Indians not to enter into any such agreement with Iran. The American logic is that the US's enemies have to be opposed by India, its 'strategic partner'. Unfortunately for the Congress, the country is in no mood to accept American dictations on foreign policy.

The Congress will be leaving the office with a baggage of failed foreign policy, and the country will have to take several steps to undo the damage done by the UPA Government's misadventures. Besides, the Congress has no one else except itself to blame for following a disastrous foreign policy because it ignored the dissenting voices from both within the party and the country. *1 May 2008, Pioneer*

With Difficult Neighbours like Pakistan and China, Asian Solidarity is Impossible

External Affairs Minister Pranab Mukherjee, in his address to the Beijing University on June 6, pleaded for the establishment of supra-country Asian group. Mukherjee said, 'An open and inclusive architecture, which is flexible enough to accommodate the great diversity which exists in Asia, is needed'. He made a plea for the creation of an Asian group which should transcend the existing dialogue forms.

Three such forms for dialogue among Asian countries are the ASEAN Regional Forum the Conference on Interaction and Confidence Building Measures in Asia and the Shanghai Co-operation Organisation. The South Asian Association for Regional Cooperation has also observers like China, Japan, South Korea, European Union and the US. India, Russia and China also hold annual conferences to discuss their common problems.

It deserves to be clearly stated that Mukherjee is talking of what Jawaharlal Nehru had dreamt as early as 1947. Nehru's belief in the realisation of his dream of Asian community was based on the premise that the whole of Asia had shared history of struggles against colonialism and such shared experience will bring all Asians together after de-colonisation. India had hosted Afro-Asian Conference in Delhi in 1947 and the Bandung Conference in Indonesia was held to evolve a common platform of Non-Aligned Asian countries in the context of the Cold War era. Nehru's dream was completely shattered when India and China, two pillars of future Non-Aligned Asia, fought a full-fledged war in 1962.

Thereafter, Nehru's dream got completely shattered when many Asian countries from Japan to Pakistan opted for American security umbrella for their territorial defence. Many Asian countries signed military pacts with one or the other superpower. Nehru's dream of all Asian Identity was replaced by a phenomenon of completely fragmented Asia and Asians against Asians became the reality of world affairs form 1945 to 1990.

The idea of decolonised Asia coming together remained a pipedream till the end of the Cold War, and it seems Mukherjee's desire to revive the idea of common Asian architecture in the 21st century will remain unfulfilled. A few facts may be mentioned to contextualise the new reality of Asia in the present American-dominated 'unipolar' system. First, the journey of decolonised, pauperised and backward Asia has come to an end and a new Asia has emerged on the global scene. East Asia, Japan, China, Taiwan,

India et al have merged as strong economic centres, instead of the Aid Dependent Asia of 1945 to 1990.

The US and the European Union are coming to terms with new emerging capitalist countries of Asia and the economic balance of power today is witnessing great shifts because the erstwhile Third World Asian countries are joining the group of relatively developing category of capitalist countries. Has the emergence of new capitalist Asia brought Asian countries closer to one another? Do these new Asian economic centres of power stand more integrated among themselves?

Every major Asian country is not only militarily strong in conventional sense, China, India, Pakistan and North Korea have become new nuclear weapon states and their strategic role with new military strength has undergone a qualitative charge in the year beginning from the 1950s to the first decade of the 21st century. Incidentally, China became the first nuclear weapon state in Asia in the 1960s and the other Asian countries like India or Pakistan or North Korea also decided to follow it. Are the three nuclear weapon states of Asia – China, India and Pakistan – candidates for Asian solidarity while maintaining their military arsenal for security from neighbouring countries? Why were the Chinese worried when India exploded nuclear device in 1998? Why did Pakistan conducted nuclear test in the wake of the Pokhran II tests? The story does not end here. Japan is a major economic power in Asia and the whole Asian continent will suffer tremendous earthquake if Tokyo decides to opt for nuclear weapon system.

Every major Asian country is accelerating its military power to safeguard its territorial integrity and national sovereignty against any threat from other Asian neighbouring state. So, Mukherjee's ideas about Asian solidarity is a non-starter if one keeps in mind the status of inter-state relations between India, Pakistan and China. If the level of mutual trust based on the principle of peaceful co-existence had been the guiding principle of these three nuclear armed neighbouring states, they could have been active promoters of the idea of common Asian security architecture.

India's baggage of problems of foreign and security problems, especially with Pakistan and China, is full of difficulties. The Asian solidarity is a pipe dream and Mukherjee must know this. *17 June 2008, Pioneer*

Encounter with Jihad: The challenge is to tackle ideologically-motivated terrorists

It is an established fact that terrorism in India has been exported from the neighbouring countries but at the same time it is also essential to take cognisance of indigenous and domestic factors which are responsible for the birth and growth of terrorism within the country. Religion-based or caste-based or region-based conflicts have also taken the form of violent confrontations among different segments of society and this fact cannot be denied that the level of social violence among groups in different parts of the country has assumed dangerous levels for democratic political system. Of late, the focus of public discourse is on the growth of violent terrorist activities undertaken by a section of religious fanatics who believe that it is their sacred religious duty to inflict pain on their religious enemies. Religion in public life is in multi-religious culturally pluralist and diverse society can become a breeding ground for the practitioners of religious-based campaigns against their 'other' religious enemies.

It is no denying that religion-based contests sometimes take the form of mindless violent terrorism. It has been a great misfortune of India that a section of religious fanatics like terrorists of Punjab in the 1980s or externally financed and supported *Jihadis* or *Taliban* of the 1990s or other religious fanatic groups have violently targeted innocent people. Further, terrorists in the name of their religion have indulged in violent activities in urban areas because it provides them with an opportunity to get publicity by the mass media, both audio and print. The 'Urban-centred terrorism' attracts instant attention because of its visibility. It is not, without reason that 'September 11, 2001 and post-September 12, terrorist attacks in every European and non-European country has been confined to urban centres because one of the goals of terrorists is to spread their message in all parts of the world.

The real challenge before the Central and the State Governments in India is to tackle the ideologically-motivated violent terrorists groups in large, medium and small cities. It deserves to be clearly stated that the Government, whether at the Centre or of the States, cannot fight ideological battles against religious fanatics who are highly motivated because they are the carriers of religious bigotry and doctrines as interpreted by them and their priestly classes.

The extreme forms of religion-based politics are preached and practiced by the leaders of religious communities and the task of countering the ideology of terrorism is also to be performed by a section of leadership who can stand up against their own religious preachers and practitioners of religious hatred. If religious doctrines are used and abused in justification of religiously motivated violent terrorist activities, such a misrepresentation of religious doctrines can be corrected and challenged only by leaders of communities and other civil society, not by any State, association or group. The governmental machinery has its limitations while dealing with the ideological content of violent terrorists but it is only the Government which has the duty and resources to confront bullets of the terrorists by the bullets of the professional armed forces of the country. KPS Gill or Julius Roberio was not religious preacher but confronted the terrorists of Punjab by following the policy of 'bullet for bullet'.

The lesson from Punjab of the 1980s is that a democratic Government has to mobilise leaders of community to counter the erroneous and misplaced religious beliefs of the practitioners of violent terrorism who are pretending to fight in defence of their religion, and make full use of its coercive power to confront guns of the terrorists by the guns of professional soldiers. This 'dual strategy' of the Government had brought peace to Punjab and only this 'dual strategy' has to be followed both by the Central and the State Governments to contain and confront the growing menace of violent terrorism. This bluff of religion-based justification for the practice of politics of religious hatred can be exposed only by political, social and cultural community leaders but the gun fire of the terrorists has to be extinguished by the powerful guns of the Government.

Post-Independence India always had extraordinary laws to meet extraordinary challenges posed by extremists of one kind or the other. The Preventive Detention Act, the Maintenance of Internal Security Act, Prevention of Terrorist Act, Unlawful Activities Act, Unlawful Laundering of Money Act, *et al*. It is not only Parliament, even many State Assemblies, subject to the assent of the President of India, have many effective laws to deal with religious extremists, even Goonda Act is quite effective in dealing with suspected miscreants. India has not been able to tackle the threats posed by terrorists in spite of the fact that Parliament has been quite cooperative in helping the execution with extra ordinary laws. The explanation for the failure of Indian Government in meeting the challenges posed by terrorism lies in its incapacity to properly use police machinery in confronting the gun power of the violent terrorists. Indian political leadership is divided in its approach to the problematic of violent terrorists. *5 August 2008, Pioneer*

Armchair Politicians can't Restore Peace in J&K

The Jammu region and the Kashmir Valley are experiencing extremely disturbed situation and the local administration of the State Government seems to have been bereaved of the options to deal with the 'sentiment' of the people who have come on the streets in defence of their demands.

The armed forces have also been deployed to handle the situation but it seems that the coercive methods adopted by the State Government and the Union Home Ministry have not borne any fruits to change the ground situation in disturbed Jammu & Kashmir. The Union Government has recognised, though quite late in the day, that the State Government has reached a dead-end and it has not only failed to manage the mess originated from the mass anger, it has become *persona non grata* with the local population. The all-party delegation led by Union Home Minister to negotiate with the protesting masses was rebuffed by the people of Jammu unless Ms Mahbooba Mufti of the PDP, Farooq Abdullah of the NC and Saifuddin Soz of the Congress were made to withdraw from the negotiating table.

The Home Minister and the representatives of other parties who went to negotiate with the local people on the land for Sri Amarnath Shrine issue should have been aware of the demand of 'boycott' by the protesting people. The situation at the ground level was much more serious than they had assessed it to be while sitting in Delhi.

Even this clear message from the protesting mass fell on deaf ears and the Prime Minister called for an all-party meeting on August 13 in Delhi. It is a very cavalier approach adopted by the Union Government because if drawing room meetings in Delhi could have led to solutions, peace would have been restored when the Home Minister led-delegation went to Jammu & Kashmir.

After the protests in Jammu for over a month now and the agitation on August 11 by the people and leaders of Valley to cross the Line of Control into Muzzafarabad to break the alleged barriers imposed by the Jammu protesters on the movement of goods from Srinagar, the ball is in the Union Government's court. The Centre and other political parties will have to actively negotiate and break the wall of distrust that has come to separate the two regions of the State. The Prime Minister, if he understands the seriousness of the situation, has himself to provide the leadership in finding a compromise solution by bringing the opposite groups around the table. Because the situation has become such grave that it is beyond the capacity of the State Government to apply any healing touch to the aggrieved people of Jammu or Kashmir.

The curfew in Jammu has been relaxed and Srinagar, after firing by the security forces on August 11, has been placed under curfew. The dispute cannot be resolved by sending interlocutors or delegations from Delhi. The Prime Minister himself should visit Jammu and Srinagar immediately and spend time and energy to assuage the bitter feelings among the people of these two regions.

Why blame Pakistan or Hurriyat for spoiling the situation and fishing in the troubled waters? If the Indian leadership is incapable of reaching out to its own people in Jammu & Kashmir, mischief-mongers will exploit the situation and further complicate matters. The Prime Minister must realise that there is nothing 'non-negotiable' in a democracy.

Further, the Prime Minister should be in direct contact with the leaders of Jammu and the Valley because at the end of the day, it is the local parties and groups which have to manage public affairs in the State. Not only this, Jammu and the Valley are burning at a time when Pakistan itself is at a crossroads and it is well-known that Pakistan 'exports' violence whenever it is facing difficulties at home.

Hence, without wasting any time, the Prime Minister should understand the gravity of the situation and involve himself directly in finding a acceptable solutions to normalise the ground situation in Jammu & Kashmir. Armchair politicians of New Delhi with no feel of the pulse of the people are bound to fail. *10 August 2008, Pioneer*

Fight Terror with Force: Government must counter the firepower of *jihadis*

It is an established fact that terrorism in India has been exported from the neighbouring countries but at the same time it is also essential to take cognisance of indigenous and domestic factors which are responsible for the birth and growth of terrorism within the country. Religion or caste or region-based conflicts have also taken the form of violent confrontations and this cannot be denied that the level of social violence among groups in different parts of the country has assumed dangerous levels for a democratic political system.

Of late, the focus of public discourse is on the growth of violent terrorist activities undertaken by a section of religious fanatics who believe that it is their sacred religious duty to inflict pain on their religious enemies. Religion in public life is in multi-religious culturally pluralist and diverse society can become a breeding ground for the practitioners of religious-based campaigns against their 'other' religious enemies.

There is no denying that religion-based contests sometimes takes the form of mindless violent terrorism. It has been a great misfortune of India that a section of religious fanatics like terrorists of Punjab in the 1980s or externally financed and supported *jihadis* or the Taliban of the 1990s or other religious fanatic groups have violently targeted innocent people of big metropolis or urban towns in various parts of the country.

Further, terrorists in the name of religion have indulged in violent activities in urban areas because it provides them with an opportunity to get publicity by the mass media. Urban-centred terrorism attracts instant attention because of its visibility. It is not without reason that September 11, 2001 and thereafter terror attacks in every European and non-European country has been confined to urban centres because one of the goals of terrorists is to spread their message in all parts of the world.

The real challenge before the Central and the State Governments in India is to tackle the ideologically-motivated violent terrorists groups in large, medium and small cities. It deserves to be clearly stated that the Government – whether at the Centre or of the States – cannot fight ideological battles against religious fanatics. The extreme forms of religion-based politics are preached and practiced by the leaders of religious communities and the task of countering the ideology of terrorism is also to be performed by a section of leadership who can stand up against their own religious preachers and practitioners of religious hatred. If religious doctrines are used and abused in justification of religiously-motivated terrorist activities, such misrepresentation of religion can be corrected and challenged only by leaders of communities and other civil society.

The Government machinery has its limitations while dealing with the ideological content of violent terrorists but it is only the Government which has the duty and resources to confront bullets of the terrorists by the bullets of the professional armed forces of the country. The lesson from Punjab of the 1980s is that a democratic Government has to mobilise leaders of community to counter the erroneous and misplaced religious beliefs of the practitioners of violent terrorism who are pretending to fight in defence of their religion, and make full use of its coercive power to confront guns of the terrorists by the guns of professional soldiers.

This bluff of religion-based justification for politics of religious hatred can be exposed only by political, social and cultural community leaders, but the firepower of the terrorists has to be extinguished by the powerful guns of the Government. Has the Government of India shown sufficient determination in confronting and liquidating the firepower of the terrorist groups? Does India lack the legal back-up and framework while facing gun-wielding terrorists?

The explanation for the failure of the Government of India in meeting the challenges posed by terrorism lies in its incapacity to properly use police machinery in confronting the firepower of terrorists. Our political leadership is also divided in its approach to the problem of terrorism. 26 *August* 2008 *Pioneer*

Pax Americana in Decline

The Fall of Berlin Wall in 1989 and the collapse of the USSR in 1991 made the US ruling classes and their political executive, represented by Presidents Reagan, Bush Sr, Clinton and Bush Jr, to impose a new global order that expressed the unlimited military and economic might of the US. It was not only the Americans, every centre of regional power – from the European Union to the emerging 'tiger' countries of South-East Asia – had accepted the hegemonic leadership of the Americans in a 'unilateral' new global order created by the post-cold war international situation.

But even before the end of the first decade of 21st century, the hegemonic military domination by the US seems to be meeting its waterloo, thanks to its misadventures in Iraq and Afghanistan. And American hegemony is gradually being eroded. The Economist recently wrote that 'now the world seems very multipolar. Europeans no longer worry about American ascendancy'. And Fareed Zakaria, a conservative, has brought out a book, The Post-American World, in which he empahsises the emergence of China and India as new centres of power.

In other words, militarist hegemonic unilaterialism of the US is on the decline and new countervailing centres of power, which have the capacity to contain the adventurism of Americans in global affairs, are emerging. Consider the following:

The Americans had assured the Indians on July 18, 2005, that President Bush would 'work with friends and allies to adjust international regime to ensure full civil nuclear energy cooperation and trade with India'. He could not carry conviction with committed non-proliferators like New Zealand, Ireland, Austria, Switzerland, Sweden, Norway, Finland and Denmark, not to forget chronic nuclear sceptics like Japan and Canada.

It should not be forgotten that all these countries, which did not agree to the US draft at the Nuclear Suppliers Group meeting held in Vienna on August 21-22, 2008, happen to be 'democracies' and it is impossible for democracies to ignore their domestic non-proliferating popular constituencies simply because a superpower like the US has decided to open the nuclear door to India.

Clearly, US hegemony, like all other hegemonies, creates its own contradictions and this is the meaning of the events of 21-22 August at Vienna meeting of the NSG. Indians should realise and recognise the fact that the so-called writ of an imperialist America does not run over the globe and it would be a mistake to 'overestimate' American global hegemony because sovereign nations, especially democratic ones, can stand up to and refuse to accept diktats, even when they come from the most powerful country in the world.

Americans have to accept that the year 2008 heralds a period that is quite different from the situation which prevailed in 1991 when Russia had collapsed, and this reminder hit home rather sharply when Georgians were taught a lesson by Russia, which clearly was not what it had been in 1991.

Russian President Dmitry Medvedev gave a 'clear warning to would-be aggressors' and he stated on August 19, 2008, that 'Russia is back as a power to be reckoned with'. An important American commentator, Paul Krugmann, wrote on August 15, 2008 in the New York Times that '...the war in Georgia is not that big a deal economically. But it does mark the end of the Pax Americana – the era in which the US more or less maintained a monopoly on the use of military force'. By attacking Georgia, Russia has challenged the whole America-led NATO military alliance.

India was not the only country that stood up to US pressures and demands at the latest WTO round of talks. WTO chief Pascal Lamy, who rushed to Delhi after the failed round of talks, stated that the world has changed from the Uruguay Round of 1995, and the WTO now has to deal with three centres of economic and trade power – the BRIC countries (Brazil, China, India and Russia), apart of course the US and EU. Can the growing economic strength of India and China be ignored at the bargaining table of not only the WTO but also similar international decision-making institutions? Lamy has observed that India, China and Brazil have emerged as 'big brothers' at global trade negotiations.

The purport of above narrative is that India is dealing with a global situation that is not only 'multipolar', but one in which the unilateralism of a hegemonic America is in decline. The experience of Indian policymakers in dealing with the bipolar cold war phase of international politics – from 1950s to 1980s – is rich. That enabled Indian policymakers to effectively deploy and leverage its foreign policy of non-alignment while dealing with power bloc and successfully safeguard our 'relative autonomy'. The multipolar global order has opened new opportunities for Indians to deal with every global centre of power, including the US, on its own terms and conditions.

If the US is not capable of playing hegemonic global role, it will not at all be possible for it to dictate 'strategic policies' pursued by India. The Indian democratic process has shown enough strength to defend its relative autonomy and freedom while dealing with multiple centres of global power and the strength of Indian democracy was best evident in the country's dogged refusal to agree to the terms and conditions on trade at the WTO, and the Manmohan Singh governments' repeated and vehement public denials that any 'conditionalities' resembling NPT or CTBT would not be accepted while concluding the civilian nuclear agreement with the US. The government and the Opposition in Indian democracy is balanced in a manner that the government cannot move even an inch without the 'consent' of the Opposition on issues of national sovereignty.

The checks and balances that operate in Indian democracy keep the government on its toes and prevents any deviation from national consensus. It is impossible for any government in India to put all its eggs in the US basket as many other centres of power – Russia, France, Japan and so on – have burst on to the global scene and India is doing business with all of them. Hence the US of 2008 is not in a position to 'dictate' conditionalities while dealing with democratic India and also stop India from dealing with other centres of multiple world order. *30 August 2008, Economic Times*

Obama will Find it Difficult to Break with the Past

Barack Hussein Obama, the new political chief executive, of the capitalist, imperialist and super-militarist state of the United States, is perceived as a forward-looking new and fresh face of the American presidency, especially as successor to the most disliked George W Bush. But is Obama really a different President and will he be able to follow a different policies than on domestic and foreign affairs? Will the Obama presidency be just a case of continuity of policies with marginal changes of a cosmetic type?

It is important to place Obama presidency in a proper context with a view to understanding the reality of the limitations under which an American President has to function. The American President, whether Republican or Democrat, functions under great restraints because the powerful, exploiting, ruling capitalist class has created a mechanism of 'lobbying' to deal with policy matters and promote the interests of different capitalist groups in the corridors of power of the US.

This is the reason that on January 22, President Obama announced the 'tightening of the rules' on 'lobbyists working in Government'. The *Economist* commented on February 3, that 'virtuously, Obama has announced that no lobbyists would serve in his Administration. Embarrassingly, he had to waive the rule immediately for two of his team'. He had to eat humble pie because he made his public commitment without understanding the iron grip which lobbyists have over the White House.

Obama has inherited serious economic recession from Bush and to get support from the Republicans in the Congress, he has appointed his Defence Secretary and Commerce Secretary from the erstwhile Republican team. This bipartisan approach is the essence of the American political system.

Obama has also followed the same strategy of a $ 819-billion bailout for approval by the American Congress. Hence, both Bush and Obama have followed the same strategy of rescuing big corporations, banks and financial institutions by offering a bailout package and both Presidents have been accused of spending tax-payers' money to help big businesses which are solely responsible for creating the present economic recession.

The real remedy for the American financial sector mismanagement is Government regulation of the unregulated and anarchic financial and banking system but Obama, like Bush, fears to governmentalise or even nationalise the sinking big banks. If Bush believed that 'free market competition and not state-directed economy' is the mantra for economic management, Obama has not dared to 'bring back the state' to cleanse the mess created by the practitioners of free market economy.

The fountain of the crisis in America is the system of unregulated financial sector but the chief political executives of the capitalist state, whether Bush or Obama, can only tinker with the existing model of free market economy, they cannot learn any new lessons and apply new remedies to deal with the serious fiscal crisis. The victims of market economics practised by Bush and Obama are the lower middle classes and Obama had to shout in public on the vulgar level of high salaries of Wall Street executives in a situation when the ranks of the unemployed are increasing.

The only difference between Bush and Obama is that of Tweedledum and Tweedledee as far as the role of the state is concerned in tackling the deep economic crisis of America which is impacting the whole world in an adverse manner, except Wall Street's millionaires and billionaires. *10 February 2009, Pioneer*

Floundering Pakistan: Nominal Democracy can't Ensure Political Stability

The post-Musharraf era has brought formal and nominal democracy back in Pakistan, but it is unlikely that it will stay right on track. A few facts may be mentioned to substantiate the argument that Pakistan will continue to remain disturbed and politically unstable as has happened during the past 60 years of that country's political journey since India was partitioned.

First, the role of the United States in overseeing the governance in Pakistan continues to be crucial and critical and nothing has changed for the Americans as far as their national interest in Pakistan is concerned. It is ironical that the US has become a votary of democracy in Pakistan. Individuals, whether military dictators or elected Prime Ministers, do not matter for the Americans because for them nothing is indispensable in Pakistani except the Army as a carrier of war against terrorism. Benazir Bhutto had agreed to all the 'conditionalities' laid down by the Americans before her entry to Pakistan from exile was cleared by General Pervez Musharraf. Asif Zardari is playing the role decided by Americans and the latest example being that the PPP-led Government has not condemned American attack on Taliban in Wazirstan which lies in the territorial boundaries of Pakistan.

Anti-American religious fundamentalists groups in Pakistan claimed to have assassinated pro-American Benazir Bhutto and also attempted an attack on Pakistan's Prime Minister on the day American forces had attacked Wazirstan. Hence, the American writ continues to run in Pakistan.

Second, the Afghanistan Government has repeatedly accused Pakistan of providing shelter to anti-Afghan terrorist groups. But all these have fell on deaf ears because the Pakistan Army continues to be a loyal ally of the Americans in their war against terrorism and the Pakistani Army Chief made his first journey abroad only to America. Benazir Bhutto had stated that the role of Army in Pakistan could not be underestimated or ignored. Third, Pakistan's fragile democratic regime is targeted by the believers of *allah* who are challenging the pro-American leadership in Pakistan, whether elected democratically or supported by the Army. The believers of *allah*, the religious fundamentalists, want to dethrone non-Taliban regime in Afghanistan and also establish real Islamic state in Pakistan.

Islamisation of Pakistani society, which in reality means freedom to the carriers of Islamic message on the basis of gun, is a direct threat to Afghanistan and India. Pakistan itself is facing threat from the Islamists and except the Army, Pakistani does not have any other institution to contain the growing menace of terrorist violence. The Islamists are a threat to the democracy in Pakistan and the stability of Pakistan is a great concern for the US and India.

Zardari and Sharif's short-lived 'coalition' has come to an end and that too on very wrong note. How can a politically divided society govern on the basis of 'national consensus' which is the need of the hour? It needs to be understood that the democratic experiment in Pakistan has repeatedly failed because the political ruling groups have refused to accept the reality of the existence of extremely powerful anti-democratic forces in their society especially represented by powerful feudal classes, Army and well-armed religious fanatic Islamist groups. How can such a society be governed democratically by divided political groups?

There is no evidence to suggest that Pakistan's elected democratic leadership has learnt any lessons from their past or they are ready to meet the new challenges. Democratically-elected political leaders have taken up personal agenda of either the reinstatement of dismissed Supreme Court judges or proposed launching of corruption cases against Sharif. The proof of pudding is in eating.

The upshot of above narration is that political developments in Pakistan should be watched very carefully because post-18 February 2008, though nominal democracy has been restored, there is no silver lining on the horizon of Pakistan. Army, *allah* and America will remain real centres of power and will continue to dominate Pakistan's domestic and external politics and the country will hover around one crisis or other. *10 September 2008, Pioneer*

It doesn't Pay to be a US Ally

India under the leadership of Prime Minister Manmohan Singh and UPA chairperson Sonia Gandhi is making conscious efforts for a 'strategic partnership' with the United States and the India-US nuclear deal is just the tip of the iceberg. But taking a cue from America's 'strategic partnership' with other countries, it is essential to highlight the meaning, significance and implications of India's newly-found love for the Americans.

Every major or minor Arab country had strategic military alliance with the US and one after the other every 'strategic ally' of America had to fight wars either with America or American outposts like Israel. The fate of Afghanistan and Iraq as the trusted friends of America is worth keeping in mind before enthusiastic Indian Government allows itself to be sucked in American scheme of strategic alliances.

Afghanistan had become a battleground between the erstwhile Soviet Union and the US-supported anti-Russian Afghan resistance groups. Incidentally, Afghanistan has not recovered from the brutal consequences of the war between the two competitors during the Cold War. Even after the withdrawal of Soviet military forces, Americans continued to support *jihadi* Afghan groups and their barbaric rule till the terrorist attacks on symbols of American power on September 11, 2001.

Pakistan has been a strategic military ally of the US irrespective of the phase of Cold War bipolar global politics or the present US-led unipolar global system. Pakistan was militarily supported by the US to checkmate India and it was with American weapons that Pakistan decided to fight India in 1965 and 1971.

Further, the US proclaimed that terrorism would be fought on a war-scale because it is a challenge to the American way of life, but it has not disciplined Pakistan which is exporting terrorist activities from its soil.

This is only one part of the story. Pakistan is completely helpless in dealing with open military interventionist operations of the US in its own territory of Waziristan. Americans have not taken even a formal consent or approval from the democratic Government in Pakistan for launching military attacks against Al Qaeda or Taliban. Strategic puppet regimes of the US are taken for granted in pursuit of Uncle Sam's own interests and goals irrespective of any impact on the sanctity or territorial integrity of the partner country. Not only this. Americans have ignored with contempt the protests against its military actions from Pakistan's Prime Minister and Army Chief because they know very well that 'strategic partners' of the US are always at their beck and call.

It is well-known that American influence penetrates in the corridors of power of its strategic allies. Like Afghanistan and Pakistan, India should be prepared to face subtle and not so subtle demands of the US in pursuing its foreign policy goals. It is not essential to go into the merits of the Iran-Pakistan-India gas pipeline, but nothing is moving forward primarily because the US has 'vetoed' this project and India is caught between the devil and the deep sea.

The country is divided on India's policy towards Iran because a perception exists that a friend's enemy has to be treated as our enemy; hence, India is going along with America's anti-Iran policy. Incidentally, Iran also has a history of military and strategic alliances with the US, and the present rupture between the two countries should not be taken at its face value.

The Government has countered the charge of new strategic alliance with the US saying the country has entered into strategic alliances with other countries as well. But India's strategic alliances with other countries do not have the same impact on our national sovereignty as a strategic alliance with the US. Can it be ignored that the India-US alliance carries absolutely different weight in international relations than that of an India-China alliance? *23 September 2008, Pioneer*

No Reason to believe America is Mindful of India's Interests

Indian middle and entrepreneurial classes have become very interested in American politics, especially in the electoral process of the United States. First, the economic integration of India in the US-led global capitalist system has made Indian industrialists, investors and professional classes stakeholders in the ups and downs faced by the US economy. The present economic recession in the US-led global economy is directly impinging on the lives of a large section of Indians and this factor has made middle and upwardly mobile middle classes to take more than a casual interest in the politics of that country.

Second, the India-US Nuclear Agreement had become a very serious and contentious debating point in our domestic politics, and the Indian middle classes, either supporters or opponents of the deal, are closely following every development linked to it. Third, the long-drawn electoral drama of the US has kept the middle classes engaged in the debate on the merits of the presidential candidates. It is not only Americans who are discussing the issue of race linked to Barack Obama's candidature; Indians are also discussing it as well as the 'dynastic issue' linked to Ms Hillary Clinton's attempt to secure the Democratic nomination. The Indian middle classes are against the prevalence of dynastic politics. The purpose of this narrative is that the literate Indian middle classes may be quite cynical about their own country's democratic process, but they are actively engaged in following every development in the US.

Unfortunately, the high level of interest shown by the Indian middle classes in American political developments is based on a very low level of understanding of the reality of 'bipartisan' politics of that country. Unlike Indian politics, American politics functions on the basis of broad national consensus, even agreement, on basic domestic and foreign policies and differences between the Democratic and the Republicans are not at all reflected on foreign policy issues or even on basic challenges facing the domestic economy. President George W Bush not only discussed, but also got full support and agreement from Obama and John McCain on his bailout proposal to pump $ 700 billion in the market to bail out the crisis ridden pillars of American economic system.

It is generally believed in India that 'neo-conservatives' represented by Bush on their own followed the aggressive policy of waging war against the Taliban regime in Afghanistan and Saddam Husain's Iraq. While the front-face of foreign policy is represented by the President, he operates on the basis of national consensus – this is more so in post-9/11 America. Not only this. Bill Clinton, even before 'neo-conservative' Bush, decided to involve Nato forces in the disintegrating process of erstwhile Yugoslavia and the Republicans had supported that war.

It is not only a question of war and peace that leads to the making of national consensus in the US, the doctrine of 'export of democracy' as an integral part of American foreign policy is supported by both the Democrats and the Republicans. The policy of 'export of democracy', even it means 'military intervention' in the domestic affairs of a country, is not a creation of Bush; Clinton also followed that policy and used Nato forces in erstwhile Yugoslavia.

This project of 'export of democracy' and 'policy of intervention' in the domestic affairs of other countries has not come to an end. McCain, writing in Foreign Affairs, has spelt out his doctrine of 'An Enduring Peace Built on Freedom' while Obama, in the same journal, has demonstrated his commitment to 'Renewing American Leadership'.

Further, it is not only Bush and Ms Condoleezza Rice who have spoken in highly laudatory tone about America's 'strategic partnership' with India while signing the India-US nuclear deal earlier this month, Obama has been extremely supportive of it. A few strong statements against Pakistan by Obama have gladdened hearts in India. Unfortunately, Indians do not understand a simple fact: Paksitan has been and will always remain a 'frontline state' for the Americans irrespective of whether a Democrat or a Republican occupies the White House.

Americans and a section of our politicians have come to the conclusion that both the US and India need each other; hence, the Americans have developed strategic relationship with our country. Mutuality of interests has brought the two countries together, and the only difference is that the US is working on the basis of 'national consensus' while dealing with India, the Indian polity is quite divided on this aspect of our foreign policy.

It is very simplistic for a section of Indians to believe that the presence of a large number of Indians in the US has begun to influence American policy towards India. It is an illusion from which many Indians in this country and the US suffer from because Indians in the US have started thinking that they are significant players in American politics like the Jews of that country. Israel is a 'very special' country in the making of American foreign policy for a very important role in a very important region for the Americans. Is India as important to the Americans as Israel?

The interest of Indians in the American presidential election should not blind them to the reality: The US is motivated only by its national interests as seen during the Cold War; it is no different in the post-Cold War phase of global politics. *21 October 2008, Pioneer*

We must Test Every Move, Every Word of Pakistan

It is a simplistic truism to state that geographically determined proximities cannot be wished away and the logic of neighbourhood has to be accepted, willingly or reluctantly, by all the South Asian countries. This is the reason that every political development or message from Pakistan deserves to be seriously analysed by the Indian policymakers.

Pakistani President Asif Ali Zardari, who seems to be making right noises, announced of late that Pakistan's Nuclear Weapon Doctrine is based on the principle that 'his country will not be the first to use nuclear weapons in any war like situation with India'. Zardari's message is that India-Pakistan should move towards 'normalcy'. Not only this. Indian Nuclear Weapon Doctrine is also based on the principle of 'No-First-use' but India does not accept Zardari's proposal of South Asian Non-Nuclear Treaty arguing that its strategic doctrines are not focussed only on Pakistan but also on nuclearised China.

This does not imply that India and Pakistan have to undertake confidence-building measures only on the issue of nuclear weapons, a large number of strategic concerns have to be addressed with demilitarisation of partitioned Kashmir being an important one.

Allaying apprehension that the erstwhile Jan Sangh and its new face the BJP are not ready to accept even the concept of limited autonomy under Article 370 of the Constitution for the governance of Indian part of Kashmir to rest former Prime Minister Atal Bihari Vajpayee who during a meeting with former Pakistani President Pervez Musharraf on January 5, 2004 openly said there was need for a resolution of the Kashmir dispute which should be acceptable to both the countries. Thus the ice was broken and major political parties especially the BJP and the Congress along with the Communists expressed desire to resolve Kashmir dispute. Notably, both India and Pakistan would have to cross many hurdles before arriving at a minimum consensus on the Kashmir issue but the process of talks between the two is not at all deadlocked. This is the real essence of Zardari's foreign policy statement and Nawaz Sharif of the PML (N), the other major political formation of Pakistan has repeatedly stated that democratic Pakistan is ready to resolve inherited disputes with India.

Here it is essential to say a big no to any foreign mediator from playing any role in finding resolution to bilateral disputes between the two countries.

The need for such a public stand against any role by any foreign countries has arisen because of President-elect Barack Obama's misplaced confidence of telling both India and Pakistan that the United States is ready, even willing, to act as a facilitator between these two countries.

Obama's foreign policy has following components: (a) To end war in Afghanistan; (b) Take Pakistan's help to liquidate Al Qaeda and Taliban with a view to establish peace in Afghanistan; and (c) Make Pakistan a 'capable' state to deal with the challenge of Taliban forces.

Pakistan, an important US 'ally' in restoring peace in Afghanistan, at present is finding its state apparatus ineffective in meeting the challenge of Taliban.

The US is following hyperactive policy within the territorial boundaries of Pakistan in its fight against Taliban as the latter has proved to be ineffective, even incapable, of facing the challenge of Taliban. The moral of the story is that Obama's national interest demands Pakistan's cooperation and support in restoring peace in Afghanistan and this requires that India and Pakistan should be made to resolve their bilateral disputes. Further, Pakistan is in serious economic trouble and it has approached the International Monetary Fund for a huge loan of more than US$ seven billion and it needs more money for its economy from it allies like the United States and China.

President Zardari came empty-handed from China as far as 'economic aid' is concerned and Pakistan is looking towards IMF and Obama for massive 'economic package' to meet the serious economic challenge.

Pakistan needs Obama's active support and assistance while US needs it for its military operations in Afghanistan. Pakistan and the US have commonality of national interests but India is a different cup of tea. India can and should, on its own, decide about the parameters of foreign and security policies towards Pakistan with a view to follow the long-term road of 'cooperation and competition' as good neighbours. The resolution of bilateral conflicts will be beneficial for both the countries and the enlightened self-interest of Indians can be the guiding force of foreign policy towards Pakistan.

Permanent hostility between the two neighbouring countries is counter-productive because such a situation can act as a brake over India's global role in the 21st century. Hence, scepticism about Zardari's announcement should be replaced by catching the bull by the horns and India should accelerate the process of confidence building with Pakistan.

India, instead of a US intervention, should approach other powerful 'constituencies' that are an integral part of decision-making in Pakistan. It will be worthwhile to engage Pakistani military leadership for finding a durable peace between India and Pakistan.

If India can continue to negotiate with China, a more difficult nut to crack, the same policy should be followed towards Pakistan. India has to follow policy of 'cooperation and competition' and 'contain' conflicts with both Pakistan and China. *2 December 2008, Pioneer*

India must Bank on Global Support to Tackle Terror

With the Mumbai attacks, terrorist groups have once again demonstrated that they follow their own rules of the game and have the capacity to choose their targets and the frequency of their strikes in our urban centres. It is also crystal clear that Pakistan's society, polity and economy are destabilised. US Secretary of State Condoleezza Rice, after her visit to India, has clearly stated: 'I think we do believe that there is evidence of terrorist involvement on Pakistani soil. Even if these were non-state actors, I believe they were operating on Pakistan soil. It is still Pakistan's responsibility to respond'. Former US State Secretary Madeleine Albright reacted on terrorist attacks on Mumbai by stating that Pakistan is an 'international migraine'.

How should India tackle to such a neighbouring threat posed by Pakistan-based terrorist groups?

While dealing with Pakistan, India has to clearly understand the reality of multiple power structures that operate within the country (Pakistan) because the capability of a state to deal with any challenge – internal or external – depends on its capacity to impose its decisions within its own territorial boundaries.

First, for democratically elected Government in Pakistan, which is not even a year old, it is difficult to establish a complete writ of its Government over other centres of power which exist as well as operate in an 'autonomous manner'. It can be unambiguously stated that the Pakistan Government suffers from multiple disabilities and is very vulnerable while dealing with entrenched centres of power.

Pakistan President Asif Ali Zardari has clearly informed the whole world about his Government's limitations to confront Pakistani-based terrorists 'on its own' and has unambiguously called for 'cooperation and coordination' among other democratic Governments to deal with the terrorist challenge posed by Pakistani-based terrorist groups.

Should India ignore the reality of Pakistan revealed by Zardari? It goes without saying that it is in India's enlightened national self-interest to strengthen the infant democratically elected Government because civil society groups in Pakistan can play their positive role against rogue terrorist groups only when it is in power.

Second, the US must be reminded that its policies in South Asia are solely responsible for the birth of terrorism which is threatening the weak and vulnerable states like Afghanistan and Pakistan and also targeting India with the weapons of Islamic religious ideology.

Third, it is of no use ignoring the fact that Pakistan itself has been a victim of terrorism and it is finding difficult to meet with terrorist challenge with its limited resources. If Pakistan had the capability to fight against terrorists on its own, it would never have allowed deep penetration of the US forces to bomb its own people in its own territory.

It can be recalled that Pakistan under former President Pervez Musharraf verbalised its protests against direct intervention of the US as it is fighting its own war on terrorism with the full sanction of the Pakistani Government, including Pakistan's powerful military Generals.

Third, neither India nor the US can turn a blind eye to the fact that Pakistan Army has always been a pre-eminent factor in the governance of the country. India should clearly mention to the US that it cannot fight a lone battle against terrorism in Pakistan without taking Pakistani Army along. Also, Pakistan is not in a situation to wriggle out because it is an internationally accepted fact that terrorist groups are based in Pakistan territory.

Revisiting old mistakes, India must remember how it celebrated the birth of an independent Bangladesh in 1971 and how military regime of the same country became a pain in its neck. Bangladesh has been a source of problems for India and the military rulers of that country have never accepted to act on the legitimate demands of a neighbour with porous border. A democratic Government has to respond to multiple voices within their own country and military regime after suppressing the voices of dissent gets busy in pursuing its own goals.

President Zardari, at least, has been a little more responsible and open than other unaccountable and non-elected centres of power in Pakistan towards India's anger on terrorist attack on Mumbai. Pakistani and Bangladeshi Armies do not operate under any domestic system of checks and balances. It is the Pakistani civilian Government which is accountable to international public opinion and this is the best way for India while dealing with it.

The thrust of above description is that democracy in Pakistan is best for India and the latter can win its battle against terrorism by involving global multilateral agencies like the United Nations Security Council as Pakistan cannot go against the collective wishes of the United Nations.

Pakistan is not strong enough to stand up against the United Nations and also afford to pay the heavy price of isolation. India's strategy has to be to keep its doors and windows open for President Zardari's Government and make every effort to actively engage the global community to Pakistan in its fight against terrorism.

India must understand that the present international support will disappear if any unilateral aggressive action is contemplated by the Government. *16 December 2008, Pioneer*

Look beyond America: A declining US can be of no help to India

The Mumbai terrorist attacks of November 26 should compel the Indian foreign and defence policy-makers to revisit the crumbling policy premises. This is because before 26/11 our policies have seldom stood the test of time during a national crisis. A few facts may be mentioned to substantiate the argument that India should revise and reorient its foreign policy, especially in the light of new challenges which have emerged before the country.

The Indian foreign policy establishment had thought that Pakistan could be isolated by the international community because India's strategic allies would be able to successfully pressurise Pakistan to help India in its fight against terrorism. The most important premise of Indian foreign policy-makers was based on the belief that the US has great 'clout' over Pakistan. And as India is a 'strategic ally of the US', Americans will exercise their influence over Pakistan in favour of India. It is essential to state here that the Vajpayee-led NDA Government had extended full support to the US after 9/11 attack. So the Manmohan Singh-led UPA Government expected that the US would declare a similar kind of war against terrorists originating from Pakistan after 26/11.

Indians were very happy when the United Nations Security Council passed a resolution to ban Jamaat-ud-Dawah and the British Prime Minister, the French and German Governments also extended active 'verbal' support to Indians against terrorist attacks from Pakistani territory. US Secretary of State Condoleezza Rice also visited India and Pakistan and issued statements saying Pakistan to act against the perpetrators of the Mumbai attacks.

The over-enthusiasm of Indian policy-makers died down quite early when Pakistan refused to be pressurised and did not cooperate with India. The pillar of the Indian foreign policy collapsed because the US and other Western countries failed to internationally isolate Pakistan. It took a long time for the policy-makers to accept that their 'strategic' partnership with the US proved an empty promise.

Pranab Mukherjee, while addressing Indian Ambassadors and

High Commissioners, shared his feelings that 'The terrorist infrastructure in Pakistan is the greatest danger to the security of the entire civilised world'. He continued: 'We have so far worked at several levels. We have sought the support of international community to put pressure on Pakistan... and we are also clear that ultimately it is we who have to deal with this problem'.

It is never too late to realise and accept that strategic alliances with the US are phoney because the US has its own national interests and it needs Pakistan for the promotion of its own goals.

Pakistan is very well defended by its tired-and-tested ally China. Post-26/11 China's statements, unlike the US, have been very guarded, cautious and even lukewarm. Our policy-makers have completely misjudged that China is a pillar of strength for Pakistan's security and defence concerns. While it appealed to India and Pakistan to maintain calm and work together to investigate the cause of the terrorist attacks on Mumbai, China needs Pakistan for the promotion and protection of its strategic and security interests in the South Asian region and Pakistan needs China's support against its mighty neighbour India.

Hence India cannot expect any solid support form China against Pakistan on the issue of terrorism and Pranab Mukherjee is wasting his time by stating that Pakistan-based terrorist groups are a threat to the world. Every country is looking at the problem of India-Pakistan discord from its own point interest and strategic alliances of India with other countries have no relevance while dealing with individual disputes.

Where does India go from here? The answer depends on India's understanding of the global situation during the second decade of the 21st century. Indians must accept that America-led unipolar international system is dead like a dodo and its global hegemony of the last two decades has come to an inglorious end. During its hegemonic phase of unipolarity has faced waterloo in Iraq and Afghanistan and all its boastful claims of 'export of democracy' have met with disastrous consequences. America's much-touted economic model of 'free market' economy has brought immense sufferings not only to its own people but also to other countries which followed that model.

America stands weakened because its economy is facing serious recession and also it has no moral standing in international relations. How can Indians expect any worthwhile support from an economically weak and militarily demoralised country in its fight against terrorism with Pakistan?

It is high time for India to look around and operate beyond an America which is on decline. Our policy-makers should be beware of President-elect Barrack Obama who is determined to wage a war in Afghanistan and he will expect India's support in the pursuit of aggressive foreign policies. We should look towards other 'centres' of power at the global level and get out of the unwanted umbrella of the United States and deal with Pakistan on the basis of its own resources and capabilities.

An independent foreign policy is the need of the hour. India has never been part of imperialist forces and this strong tradition of post-Independence phase of foreign policy should be vigorously pursued and it is possible only if Indians are perceived as independent actors in world affairs. This is the need of the second decade of the 21st century. *30 December 2008, Pioneer*

We shouldn't Stop Talking to Pakistan

Prime Minister Manmohan Singh while addressing the Chief Ministers on January 5 completely rejected Pakistan's argument that 'non-state actors' might have been responsible for the terrorist attack on Mumbai on November 26 last year. The Prime Minister observed that the attacks were a handiwork of Pakistan-based outfit Laskhar-e-Tayyeba and there is enough evidence to show that, given the sophistication and military precisions of the attack, it must have had the support of some official agencies in Pakistan.

The Prime Minister for the first time clearly and unambiguously held Pakistan fully accountable for the attack in Mumbai. It is not only that the 'state-actors' who are directly involved in such nefarious activities, he stated that Pakistan has used terrorism as an instrument of state policy. The 'managers' of Pakistan state were completely rattled as Singh had put the state agencies in the dock and the only available escape route for them was to deny everything which has been stated or made available to them on the basis of evidence.

How does India deal with a hostile neighbour like Pakistan? The whole democratic and secular social fabric of India is threatened by a neighbouring country because the export of terrorism by Pakistani is bound to bring retaliatory responses from the victims of terrorism. First, war between these two nuclear-armed countries is not at all an option and, in spite of the rhetoric of Pakistani leadership, the option of war is just ruled out because neither India has talked of war against Pakistan nor powerful global countries can remain passive spectators to any war between India and Pakistan. The Pakistanis may not be against international dictations in disputes between these two countries, Indians can not tolerate the role of outsiders in our policymaking.

Second, Indians should recognise the limitations of outsiders in resolving our bilateral disputes because every nation makes its own calculations while dealing with international or regional or sub-regional disputes and conflicts. India has provided evidence on the Mumbai terrorist attack to all the major countries which can influence Pakistan and it makes no sense for Home Minister P Chidambaram to travel to the US. The US FBI is actively involved in the investigation. India has as well provided evidence to China and Arab countries, especially Saudi Arabia, which has a clout over Pakistan. But the history and politics of Arab countries clearly tells us that it is useless for the Government to expect from the Arab countries to play positive role in making Pakistan act as a responsible neighbour of India.

India has rightly performed its duty by sharing with the world community about the existence of terrorist factory in Pakistan, but nothing should be expected from the US or China or Arab countries because they have limited role in the resolution of bilateral hostilities in this region of South Asia.

India has to break the ice by finding its own solutions to this serious challenge from Pakistan. A 'fragile' political system is a liability for a neighbour because extremely contradictory responses are bound to emerge from such a political system. A 'fragile' state is always under domestic pressures and its every decision can be reversed because some powerful lobby is opposed to that particular decision. The Government of Pakistan could not decide on the issue of sending ISI chief to India and it was clear that within Pakistan there was no one authoritative centre of power whose decision on the issue of sending the ISI chief could be taken as final. National Security Advisor of Pakistan Mohammad Ali Durrani was sacked on January 8 because he had confirmed the Indian allegation that Ajmal Amir Kasab was a Pakistani national. Is Durrani a victim of feud between Prime Minister Yousaf Raza Gilani and President Asif Ali Zardari?

The above facts clearly substantiate the analysis of Prime Minister Manmohan Singh because 'fragility' of the Pakistani state has made the dialogue process quite difficult. Hence, it is essential to keep such uncertainties of state behaviour in mind and accept the suggestion of Pakistan that both India and Pakistan should jointly investigate the terrorist attack on Mumbai. India should take Pakistan's offer of 'joint investigation' at its face value and both the countries should jointly launch investigation in a time-bound frame. The logic of a 'fragile' state system like that of Pakistani is that every offer or suggestion from that country should be taken up by the Indian Government while keeping in mind that every such 'offer' is tentative because someone else in Pakistan may veto the idea of 'joint investigations'.

The 'dialogue' between India and Pakistan on every contentious issue cannot be undertaken on the basis of a really fixed agenda but it is always worthwhile to engage Pakistan in negotiations even at a minimalist level. India has only two options while dealing with Pakistan: Dialogue or deadlock. India's efforts to urge the international community for support on the issue of terrorism from Pakistani soil and its direct role in the export of terrorism is bound to have very limited results. The so-called international community could not stop American aggression against Iraq or the ongoing

Israeli war in the Gaza Strip. On the other hand dialogue with Pakistan also cannot guarantee any positive results but this is the best option available to India. *13 January 2009, Pioneer*

Continue Dialogue: We shouldn't stop talking to Pakistan

Prime Minister Manmohan Singh while addressing the Chief Ministers on January 5 completely rejected Pakistan's argument that 'non-state actors' might have been responsible for the terrorist attack on Mumbai on November 26 last year. The Prime Minister observed that the attacks were a handiwork of Pakistan-based outfit Laskhar-e-Tayyeba and there is enough evidence to show that, given the sophistication and military precisions of the attack, it must have had the support of some official agencies in Pakistan.

The Prime Minister for the first time clearly and unambiguously held Pakistan fully accountable for the attack in Mumbai. It is not only that the 'state-actors' who are directly involved in such nefarious activities, he stated that Pakistan has used terrorism as an instrument of state policy. The 'managers' of Pakistan state were completely rattled as Singh had put the state agencies in the dock and the only available escape route for them was to deny everything which has been stated or made available to them on the basis of evidence.

How does India deal with a hostile neighbour like Pakistan? The whole democratic and secular social fabric of India is threatened by a neighbouring country because the export of terrorism by Pakistani is bound to bring retaliatory responses from the victims of terrorism. First, war between these two nuclear-armed countries is not at all an option and, in spite of the rhetoric of Pakistani leadership, the option of war is just ruled out because neither India has talked of war against Pakistan nor powerful global countries can remain passive spectators to any war between India and Pakistan. The Pakistanis may not be against international dictations in disputes between these two countries, Indians can not tolerate the role of outsiders in our policymaking.

Second, Indians should recognise the limitations of outsiders in resolving our bilateral disputes because every nation makes its own calculations while dealing with international or regional or sub-regional disputes and conflicts. India has provided evidence on the Mumbai terrorist attack to all the major countries which can influence Pakistan and it makes no sense for Home Minister P Chidambaram to travel to the US. The US FBI is actively involved in the investigation. India has as well provided evidence to China and Arab countries, especially Saudi Arabia, which has a clout over Pakistan. But the history and politics of Arab countries clearly tells us that it is useless for the Government to expect from the Arab countries to play positive role in making Pakistan act as a responsible neighbour of India.

India has rightly performed its duty by sharing with the world community about the existence of terrorist factory in Pakistan, but nothing should be expected from the US or China or Arab countries because they have limited role in the resolution of bilateral hostilities in this region of South Asia.

India has to break the ice by finding its own solutions to this serious challenge from Pakistan. A 'fragile' political system is a liability for a neighbour because extremely contradictory responses are bound to emerge from such a political system. A 'fragile' state is always under domestic pressures and its every decision can be reversed because some powerful lobby is opposed to that particular decision. The Government of Pakistan could not decide on the issue of sending ISI chief to India and it was clear that within Pakistan there was no one authoritative centre of power whose decision on the issue of sending the ISI chief could be taken as final. National Security Advisor of Pakistan Mohammad Ali Durrani was sacked on January 8 because he had confirmed the Indian allegation that Ajmal Amir Kasab was a Pakistani national. Is Durrani a victim of feud between Prime Minister Yousaf Raza Gilani and President Asif Ali Zardari?

The above facts clearly substantiate the analysis of Prime Minister Manmohan Singh because 'fragility' of the Pakistani state has made the dialogue process quite difficult. Hence, it is essential to keep such uncertainties of state behaviour in mind and accept the suggestion of Pakistan that both India and Pakistan should jointly investigate the terrorist attack on Mumbai. India should take Pakistan's offer of 'joint investigation' at its face value and both the countries should jointly launch investigation in a time-bound frame. The logic of a 'fragile' state system like that of Pakistani is that every offer or suggestion from that country should be taken up by the Indian Government while keeping in mind that every such 'offer' is tentative because someone else in Pakistan may veto the idea of 'joint investigations'.

The 'dialogue' between India and Pakistan on every contentious issue cannot be undertaken on the basis of a really fixed agenda but it is always worthwhile to engage Pakistan in negotiations even at a minimalist level. India has only two options while dealing with Pakistan: Dialogue or deadlock. India's efforts to urge the international community for support on the issue of terrorism from Pakistani soil and its direct role in the export of terrorism is bound to have very limited results. The so-called international community could not stop American aggression against Iraq or the ongoing Israeli war in the Gaza Strip. On the other hand dialogue with Pakistan also cannot guarantee any positive results but this is the best option available to India. *13 January 2009, Pioneer*

Signals from Islamabad: A weak Pakistan has surrendered to taliban; let's not push it

The ice was broken and the first response from Pakistan to India was received on February 12 in which Islamabad accepted that the terrorist attacks on Mumbai on November 26, 2008, had originated from Pakistani soil. The US Ambassador in India, David C Mulford, immediately reacted to Pakistan's acknowledgement that terrorist attack on Mumbai was 'launched from Pakistan' and he said it was an 'important first step in the right direction' and the US would 'watch and help'.

A day later, on February 13, Minister for External Affairs Pranab

Mukherjee said, 'We are at a point in our relationship where the authorities in Pakistan have to choose the kind of relationship that they want with India in the future. Much depends on actions in the Mumbai case reaching their logical conclusion'. He said while Pakistan's 'admission' was a 'positive development', normalcy in bilateral relations cannot be restored and the ongoing 'composite dialogue' between the two countries was definitely 'at a pause'. The Government of Pakistan had to do much more to assure India that the perpetrators of the heinous crime in Mumbai would be really punished and till then 'normalcy' in bilateral relations could wait.

It deserves to be clearly stated that the chapter on post-Mumbai cannot be easily closed because India has not only internationalised the issue, many foreign countries have come out in open support of India's case against Pakistan. US President Barack Obama has appointed Richard Holbrooke as his special envoy: After visiting Afghanistan and Pakistan, he said in Delhi on February 16, 'Your country, Pakistan and the US all face an enemy that poses direct threat to our leaderships, our capitals and our people'.

The real meaning of internationalisation of Pakistan's role by India on the issue of terrorism is that an extremely balanced approach should be followed by India towards Pakistan. India should not forget that Pakistan is facing serious internal threat from the Taliban and Al Qaeda and these religious fanatics are not only creating problems for India, they are also destabilising the state of Pakistan. It will be foolhardy on the part of India to ignore the disturbed domestic situation prevailing in Pakistan because Pakistan's responses towards India will be coloured and conditioned by its domestic situation.

A few serious domestic developments within Pakistan may be mentioned here. President Asif Ali Zardari said on February 14, 'We are aware of the fact that the Taliban (is) trying to take over the state of Pakistan... We have weakness and they are taking advantage of that weakness... So, we are fighting for the survival of Pakistan. We are not fighting for the survival of anyone else'. Skeptics in

India have dismissed Zardari's statement because in the past, Pakistan has made many statements with a view to getting out of difficult international situations created by its own religious fanatic groups.

However, the statement of February 14 was not hollow because the Army-led state of Pakistan completely surrendered before the Taliban and on February 17 it agreed to the imposition of shari'ah as demanded by the Taliban and Al Qaeda in the Swat Valley in the tribal area of the North-West Frontier Province. The Pakistani Government agreed to create a state within a state and the Pakistani state agreed to vacate its own territory and hand over governance to fanatics.

The Pakistani state has surrendered before religious fanatics not because of any external or international pressure, but because it has no capacity to take on and confront the Taliban. The Pakistani state has proved its weakness while dealing with well-armed religious fanatics. The authority of the Pakistani state has been compromised because in one part of the country qazi courts will implement shari'ah and in other parts the courts established by the state will administer justice according to the Pakistani Constitution.

India must realise that a weak and vulnerable state of Pakistan cannot face internal destabilisers who are represented by theologians and clerics. A theocratic state of Pakistan can become a permanent enemy of the democratic, pluralist and secular state of India, and bilateral relations between a theocratic versus a secular state cannot be normal. Thus the major challenge to Indian security has come from religious destabilisers and the real goal of these fanatics is to establish a theocratic state of Pakistan. Such a state will be permanently involved in anti-India aggressive policies.

Pakistan is unable to control its own creation and anti-India terrorists created by Pakistan are ready to destroy and take over complete control of the Pakistani state. As a result, Pakistan finds itself in a situation where if it cannot crush its own creation – the religious fanatics – these groups will take over the power of the Pakistani state. It is a new challenge for Indian public policy-makers and they have to evolve new strategies to tackle the new developments in Pakistan.

First, Mukherjee, in his well-considered response, said on February 18 that Pakistan has admitted that its soil was used by terrorists for their operation on November 26; that 'war with Pakistan will not solve the problem of terrorism'; and, that despite the signals coming from Pakistan, 'we do not have to rub them on the wrong side. We understand the complexities (in Pakistan)'. These comments amount to a very clear approach towards Pakistan.

Mukherjee has noted that the agreement arrived at with the Taliban on imposing shari'ah reveals the serious weaknesses of the Pakistani state to contain the menace of a religion-inspired violent movement. It is not at all in India's interest to humiliate a neighbouring country and this was precisely Mrs Indira Gandhi's attitude towards Pakistan after the creation of Bangladesh in 1971.
25 February 2009, Pioneer

Stabilising South Asia: Countries need to solve problems together

The security concerns of every South Asian country are determined and decided by major upheavals or disturbances within its neighhoburing countries. The implication of this logic of interdependence cannot be ignored by policy-makers of any country of the region and this fact had led to the formation of South Asian Association of Regional Cooperation. However, this experiment of regional cooperation has not worked effectively as different countries in the region are at logger-heads with one another. A few recent developments in South Asia may be highlighted to substantiate the argument that bilateral and multilateral contentious issues continue to adversely impact its stability.

First, the 26/11 Mumbai attacks created a feeling of anger against Pakistan which was suspected to be behind it. India has been worried about some important political developments taken place in Pakistan which have politically divided and weakened the authority of the Pakistani state. On the one hand, American Air Force Planes are bombarding the places of sanctuary of *jihadis* while on the other, the Pakistani state has agreed to cede its own authority in the Swat Valley by conceding the right of the Taliban to govern as per Islamic laws. A theocratic state of Pakistan is a challenge to the democratic secular state of India.

Moreover, the so-called democratic forces in Pakistan are completely divided and instead of dealing with the challenges posed by gun-wielding Islamic forces, PML(N) chief Nawaz Sharif and Pakistan Prime Minister Asif Ali Zardari are fighting their own battles. Completely divided and fragile democratic forces cannot effectively deal with the challenge of Islamist forces within their own country. The terrorist attack on the Sri Lankan cricket team on March 3, 2009 in Lahore corroborates that terrorists have turned against their own creators within the Pakistani establishment.

With the withering away of the authority of the Pakistani state, terrorists will be tools in the hands of the Pakistani Army and the ISI. It is difficult for India to 'negotiate' with a weak and ineffective democratic Government of Pakistan.

Second, a new area of concern for the Indian security establishment is Bangladesh which witnessed a mutiny in the Bangladesh Rifles on February 25 and 26, just two months after Sheikh Hasina assumed office as Prime Minister. Although External Affairs Minister Pranab Mukherjee had visited Bangladesh after rest ration of democracy, it is time India concentrates on the security of its own porous borders. A lot is expected from democratic regime in Bangladesh but even before Shiekh Hasina could settle down her authority has been challenged by anti-democratic forces. She has expressed her feelings by stating that such small mutinies are expected in the future.

Third, the ongoing civil war in Sri Lanka has serious implications not only on the security of India but also on Tamil Nadu politics and society. The Centre cannot ignore the sentiments of Tamil Nadu because a section of population is not only sympathetic towards the Liberation Tigers of Tamil Elam but also mounting pressure on it to act.

India had established stable relationship with pre-Maoist regimes in Nepal and suddenly a new situation arose in the Himalayan country, which demands new response from it.

The Governments of all these countries are involved in internal disputes which have a direct bearing on the domestic and foreign policies of India. An interlocked South Asia cannot only talk of assets of regional integration, the region as a whole has to pay heavy price for all the upheavals which have been occurring quite frequently in these countries. In the wake of the above discussion about the relatively disturbed situation prevailing in the countries of South Asia and in the light of their inter-country repercussions, it is essential to think ahead for finding some institutional solutions to the problems faced by it.

After all, divided Europe, after great efforts, could establish a European Union for collective action and decision-making on issues concerning the whole of region. South East Asia has also succeeded in establishing Common supra-state organisation like ASEAN for deliberations and decisions on common problems facing East Asia. It was hoped that the establishment of South Asian Association for Regional Cooperation would provide an opportunity to all the member countries to work with consensus and evolve common solutions to common challenges. Unfortunately, the SAARC has not shown any potential for providing a common direction. The Foreign Ministers Conference of the SAARC countries in Colombo in February 2009, did not attract even media comments as India was busy talking with Pakistan about 26/11 attacks and related issues.

It is not that the Governments in South Asia are incapable of realising the merits of creating effective common institutional arrangement for achieving commonality of goals. Then why cannot these countries pool their resources to investigate common problems facing the region instead of heading for the West? It is not denied that inter-country disputes in the South Asian region are quite serious but it is also a fact that no country can remain immune to any upheaval in the neighbouring country. This is a hard reality of South Asia and real solutions will have to be found at a collective regional level only. Otherwise, we will all sink together. The need of the hour is to swim together. *17 March 2009, Pioneer*

Beware of American Policies

As Indian and American strategic interests in the region have no meeting ground, we should try to iron out differences with Pakistan at the bilateral level and without the involvement of the US

It must be extremely flattering for a pro-American lame duck Manmohan Singh Government to be told by the US that India has to play a 'critical role' in the Afghanistan-Pakistan policies pursued by the US. The present Government should keep in mind that the new AfPak strategic doctrine of the Obama Administration demands careful thinking and analysis. Further, the outgoing Government has no right to commit the future Government post-Lok Sabha election on policy options to be exercised by the nation. However, the Obama Administration is in a hurry to 'implement' its new strategic doctrine in AfPak region and this urgency has been expressed of late by Afghanistan-Pakistan US Special Envoy Richard Holbrooke in New Delhi.

Holbrooke and US Chairman of the Joint Chiefs of Staff, Admiral Mike Mullen, have elaborated new strategic doctrine by stating that 'regional problems require regional solutions', and hence 'We cannot settle Afghanistan and many other world problems without India's full involvement'. The Obama Administration wants to build India-US relations on the solid foundations laid down by former Presidents Bill Clinton and George W Bush and it has acknowledged that India and US have developed best economic and diplomatic relationship with each other, and time has come to engage India in 'global and regional strategic' problems so that it can play its legitimate leadership role.

Holbrooke observed that 'In the entire process, we never involved India in global and strategic issues... we came to accelerate that'.

The message from the Obama Administration to India is that it is in the common interest of America, Pakistan, Afghanistan and India to adopt common strategies to confront and fight against Al Qaeda and the Taliban because these religious fundamentalist organisations pose threat to all of them. India has been a victim of terrorists who may be from Afghanistan but are exported to India from Pakistan. Hence, the first foreign and strategic priority of India is not to rescue Afghanistan from the threats of the Taliban but to confront terrorist groups which are patronised by Pakistan.

Hence, India and Pakistan, without the involvement of the US or any outside power, should try to sort out issues at the bilateral levels only. Bilateralism is the only strategic doctrine of India while dealing with challenges which emerge from Pakistan. However, the 26/11 Mumbai attack has disrupted the 'mutual confidence building' launched by the two neighbouring countries.

The Indian Government post-26/11 has not talked of America or Afghanistan; it has only singled out Pakistan by stating that it has to accept pre-conditions for any future meaningful dialogue. While bilateralism is the keyword in India's foreign policy towards Pakistan, for the US, Afghanistan and Pakistan are interrelated strategic issues because the primary concern of Washington is to liquidate the Taliban in Afghanistan for which it needs Pakistan, as it thinks that the latter is equally concerned about the nefarious role of the Taliban who have safe sanctuaries in Pakistan.

Developing peaceful relations with Afghanistan is what India is interested in. However, it cannot play any role in defending the latter militarily against the Taliban because India's primary concern should be Pakistan's role in the export of terrorism.

Indian and American strategic interests in the region have no meeting ground. Not only this, it's hardly comforting for India to learn that there are 'good' and 'bad' Taliban because religious fanatics are above any rationality and only the US has the special yardstick instrument to measure who is good and who is bad Taliban. Further, the US is providing a lot of financial aid to Pakistan and the friends of Pakistan in Tokyo are also deciding about providing it financial support. It is between the US and Pakistan to help one another in their strategic goals.

Americans have decided to deploy 17,000 armed forces in Afghanistan and it is expected that Nato countries would also participate militarily to fight the Taliban and it is up to Pakistan to become an ally of the Western military project. It deserves to be clearly stated that it is not for the first time that Pakistan has decided to act on behalf of Western military project of one kind or the other.

With past experiences, India knows that the US's advice has always been 'free' but once it comes to action, America only pursue its own interests in the regional conflicts. Further, India has enough capability to deal with the threats posed by terror outfits like Lakshar-e-Tayyeba, Taliban, Al Qaeda or others masquerading as freedom fighter in Jammu & Kashmir. The US must remember that from Vietnam to Iraq, it has never won any war and Afghanistan could be a Waterloo for Barack Obama as Iraq was for George W Bush.

The tried and tested foreign policy options pursued by India should be to keep Pakistan engaged in bilateral negotiations and keep external interlocutors out of it. It is a slow path for finding solution to old disputes, but this is a better way of reaching Pakistan than getting sucked in Obama's AfPak strategic doctrine.

Pakistan has no problems with America. It can always barter away its sovereignty for American aid and execute American doctrines but India is not in that league. *15 April 2009, Pioneer*

5

Elections: Lok Sabha 2009

A Weak and Flawed Foundation

The Indian ruling classes and their political representatives are justifiably proud that the country has managed to build an army of highly educated and skilled technocratic and professional groups through essentially its own indigenous educational institutional system. Unsurprisingly, they advocate that these social assets be further consolidated and towards this end have planned large investments for expanding the capacity of high quality educational institutions in the field of science, technology and management studies. In pursuing this strategy, India is only following the footsteps of other class-divided advanced capitalist societies that quality educational institutions are meant for those who can afford an expensive higher education on the basis of their class status and the children of poor and the marginal strata of society should remain satisfied with indifferent and basic schooling. They conveniently forget that a democratic welfare state should also try to meet the educational and social needs of children of the marginal strata who cannot afford entry to educational institutions. The Indian Constitution, in chapter IV of the Directive Principles of State Policy had clearly articulated that 'compulsory elementary and primary education will be provided to every child born in independent India'. Yet it is only sixty years later, towards the end of 2008, that the Union Cabinet finally approved the Right to Education Bill making education mandatory for children in the age group of six to 14 years. Even this step was taken six years after the 86th Constitutional Amendment of 2002 making 'free and compulsory education to all children of 6 to 14 years of age a fundamental right'.

The sad fact is that though the Indian state has the necessary resources to eradicate mass illiteracy and ensure decent schooling for all, probably since the children of the better-off have opted for 'expensive and quality private schools', education for the masses continues to be neglected. Despite the many schemes such as the Sarva Shiksha Abhiyan (SSA), National Programme for Education of Girls at Elementary Education (NPEGEE), Kasturba Gandhi Balika Vidyalaya (KGBV) or the National Programme of Mid-day Meals in schools, both the Economic Survey (2007-08) and the performance audit report by the Comptroller and Auditor General's office make evident that progress towards achieving 'education for all' remains patchy and limited.

A recent report, 'Elementary Education in India 2006-07' by Arun C. Mehta reveals that though enrolment at both primary and upper primary levels in schools has substantially increased, a vast majority of underprivileged students continue to access poorly equipped and ill-serviced government and government aided schools. A few facts drawn from Mehta's report substantiate the argument that neither quantity nor quality of education is ensured by the government. First, there are about 514 thousand para-teachers, constituting around ten per cent of the total number of teachers. The percentage of such schools is very high in Rajasthan, Madhya Pradesh and Chhattisgarh and these teachers who are purely temporary and on contractual basis, are the custodians of education for the poor children. These 'para shikshaks' who are on contract basis only receive a salary of Rs. 3000, while regular teacher earn Rs. 15,000 per month. When in desperation 80,000 such teachers of Jharkhand went on strike from 1 November 2008, the education minister responded, 'If they don't call off their strike before November 10, we will invoke the appropriate law to deal with them'. How can teachers who are themselves on tenterhooks impart any education?

Second, Mehta points out that 'with the possible exception of Daman and Diu, none of the other states have provided a *pucca* building to all its primary schools'. Further, he points to the phenomenon of 'single-classroom' and 'single-teacher' for many primary and upper primary students. Is it surprising then that the dropout rate of children enrolled in such schools remains high? Even if the official claim that the retention rate was 70.26 per cent in 2005-07 is accepted, the goal of universal retention at the primary level remains unfulfilled. Third, since the primary and upper primary level of education for children is completely 'teacher-centred', it should be of great concern to all concerned citizens that nearly half the teachers who impart elementary education in the country have themselves not studied beyond the higher secondary level and that too in secondary schools of rather indifferent quality. The same is true of the para-teachers who are engaged in providing primary education to the poorest of India.

The Arjun Sengupta report on the unorganized sector points out that, 'When 92 per cent of the country's workforce is employed in the informal or unorganized economy (i.e. those who work in the unorganized sector), it is but natural that there is a high congruence between the poor and the vulnerable segments of the society who may be called the common people'. The children of this strata of society need an active intervention and participation of the government for educational opportunities. Unfortunately, for the millions of rural and urban migrants working in the 'unorganized sector' as construction workers and in other allied daily wage linked tasks, their children are completely left out of the catchment area of the government aided educational system.

If at one level such a colossal failure of government agencies in the field of elementary and primary education for children has led to a proliferation of expensive 'private' schools, the resultant vacuum has been filled up by the emergence of denominational or sectarian schools where children are imparted education which is antithetical to the philosophy of our democratic secular Constitution. In particular, we need to pay greater attention to RSS-run Saraswati Shishu Mandirs or the Ekal Vidayalays (one-teacher primary schools). To take one example, in western Orissa alone, the Vishwa Hindu Parishad has set up '390 Hindu Ekal Vidyalayas and 50 orphanages' to impart education imbued with Hindu ideology among the impressionable children. The Sangh Parivar's Vanavasi Kalyan Ashram is very active in spreading a network of such schools in the tribal belt from Rajasthan, Madhya Pradesh, Chhattisgarh, Orissa and Jharkhand. Vidya Bharti, an all-India organization of the RSS, has established 30,000 schools, employs 80,000 teachers and close to three million children study in such schools. The story does not end here. Hindutva ideology is also spread through textbooks published by the RSS-run Sarasawti Shishu Mandir Prakashan and Vidya Bharati Publications (for details, see Aditya Mukerjee et. al., *RSS, School Texts and The Murder of Mahatma Gandhi*, Sage, 2008.)

The Sachar Commission has documented the colossal neglect of education for Muslim children by the government and how the space has been occupied by *madrasas*. Even in the national capital, Delhi, more than 1,000 madrasas continue to provide Islamic education to Muslim children. It is a pipedream to expect that secular state and society in India can be established on the basis of faith-based education imparted to millions of children in Hindu and Muslim schools. In his seminal essay, 'On Education', the philosopher Bertrand Russell stated that schools which cater to only male or only girl or only white or only black children create stereotyped images about '*the other*' and such children develop an attitude of negativism or indifference to the 'others' with whom they have not interacted in 'mixed schools'. This is happening in India. Children from Shishu Niketans or Bal Bharatis or madrasas develop great 'social distance' from other communities because in RSS-managed schools, children grow up only with other Hindus and have no contact with children of 'other religions'. Similarly in madrasas, the teacher is Muslim (cleric), the student is Muslim and education is around Koranic teachings. Can India ever build a secular society in such a situation?

It is time that civil society turns its attention to these disturbing trends. In remaining satisfied with the education available to its children while continuing to turn a blind eye to the government's neglect of quality education for the masses, we are only betraying the vision of India imbued in our democratic and secular Constitution. *December, 2008, Seminar 592*

Sonia, the Cautious Centrist

Now that the term of the UPA government is coming to a close, it is probably educative to look at the role of the chairperson of the United Progressive Alliance. She has been responsible for the survival and smooth functioning of the Congress-led UPA coalition government at the Centre.

It was for the first time in the history of post-Independence polity that the 'de facto pre-eminent' leader of the coalition government at the Centre herself had nominated someone else to be the prime minister of the country.

Sonia Gandhi was brutally attacked by the BJP-led opposition for playing the role of an extra-constitutional centre of power and without taking up the actual responsibilities of running the government. (It is another matter that the BJP governments at the Centre and the states have always operated under the extra-constitutional authority of the RSS.)

Many doubts too were expressed on the nature of the working relationship between Prime Minister Manmohan Singh and Congress president and UPA leader Sonia Gandhi who had decided to remain outside the formal arrangements of the constitutional democratic system of governance. Indians had never experienced such a 'dual system' of authority in the country. Hence, all eyes were fixed on Sonia's role in actually managing the UPA coalition government led by her own nominee prime minister.

The first challenge faced by Sonia came from senior leaders of her own party who felt cheated because in spite of their publicly proclaimed 'loyalty' to the Nehru-Gandhi family, they had been denied the coveted job of primeministership. Natwar Singh, the former foreign minister, had made it publicly known that he alone, and not PM Manmohan Singh, made foreign policy and as a great 'loyalist' he had direct access to Sonia.

A few other so-called 'loyalists' within the Congress hierarchy conveyed the message that their real leader was Sonia and not the prime minister of India. It deserves to be clearly stated that Sonia Gandhi nipped in the bud the internal critics more than once, and when required made a pubic assertion that Manmohan Singh was her party's prime minister.

Not only this, she publicly stated there will ne no deputy prime minister from the Congress in the UPA government. Dr Singh was accepted as PM by the Congress party when it became clear to all self-appointed aspirants to the post that Sonia was fully backing the PM's actions and authority.

Another serious challenge before Sonia was the task of managing a difficult coalition of fourteen parties and groups and the Left supporting the UPA from outside. Communist supporters, and her party's opponents were confident that the UPA will collapse like a house of cards because neither the Congress nor Sonia had any experience of running a coalition government at the Centre.

Moreover, Sonia was expected to manage the 'contradictions and conflicts' which are inherent in a coalition while she herself was not formally and constitutionally associated with the UPA government. How could she deal with the problems of coalition by keeping herself in the background and out of the formal government system? This was a real test for Sonia's leadership. The UPA government has not been wrecked because Sonia successfully managed the affairs by following a centrist politics and cautious approach.

A few facts may be mentioned to substantiate the argument that Sonia's centrist approach to politics is responsible for the success of the UPA coalition experiment from 2004 to 2009. First, Sonia showed a sense of 'accommodation' for the views of more than sixty Communist MPs, who were the outside supporters of the UPA coalition.

The Communists were opposed to the economic and foreign policies of Manmohan Singh, and Sonia acted as a great reconciler of the viewpoints of the two opposite poles of the coalition. She took more than two years to push for the India-US Nuclear Agreement and during this time every section of public opinion, opposition parties and UPA allies, were fully engaged in discussing the pros and cons of the agreement.

Second, the allegation that Sonia-led Congress does not know the significance of 'coalition dharma' was disproved: except for Telegana Rashtra Samiti, not a single coalition partner of the UPA has walked out because of any arrogance of power shown by Congress. The UPA coalition has continued to remain intact because Sonia has followed 'cautious centrist policies. By avoiding extreme positions she averted any situation where 'allies' felt the need to walk out of the coalition.

Further, the cautious and centrist leadership of Sonia was not only visible in the management of coalition, Congress party under her leadership made every effort to maintain the social equilibrium in spite of many serious challenges faced by the UPA government.

Atal Bihari Vajpayee provided a protective umbrella to the Narendra Modi government in 2002 when more than 2,000 Muslims were massacred in Gujarat and the BJP prime minister did not deem it essential to deal with a situation where Indian Constitution was fully violated. The UPA government, unlike its predecessor the NDA government, made every effort to maintain social harmony in the face of serious terrorist attacks from Jaipur to Mumbai.

The secular credentials of Sonia-led UPA government were fully tested in every city where terrorist violence was not allowed to take an anti-Muslim communal turn as it had happened in Gujarat in March 2002 under the Vajpayee-Modi dispensation. Sonia's Congress maintained social equilibrium and peace by following its agenda of secularism.

It also followed the same path of cautious centrist policies in the management of the economy. The die-hard economic reformers and political groups opposed to Manmohan Singh's economic policy were managed in a manner that extreme pitfalls of economic adventurism or conservatism were avoided and the middle path adopted.

The upshot of above narration is that a politically untested Sonia has proved her leadership capabilities under the most challenging context of Indian politics. Even as she remained outside the formal system, she could successfully resolve contradictions by following cautious, centrist and secular politics form 2004 to 2009. *17 January 2009, Economic Times*

Prime Ministers in the Making

It is inherent in the logic of a highly fragmented and competitive party system that leaders of multiple regional groups and parties will make it a point to project themselves as candidates for the coveted office of the prime minister. Further, this rat race among the contenders and claimants for the most important office under the parliamentary system has become quite intense especially in the run-up to the forthcoming Lok Sabha elections of April-May 2009.

Mayawati, the BSP supremo, was the first to set the cat among the pigeons by publicly claiming that she was the consensus prime ministerial candidate of the Left-floated non-Congress and non-BJP third alternative. Prakash Karat, the general secretary of the CPI(M) and the prime mover of the idea of an alternative immediately issued a disclaimer and stated that this decision will be taken collectively only after the elections. Karat did not want to commit his party to the idea of Mayawati as prime minister because alliance partners like Jayalalithaa or Chandrababu Naidu or any other dark horse may jump into the fray and claim leadership of the third front.

Sharad Pawar of the National Congress Party and Ramvilas Paswan, the Dalit leader from Bihar, who are presently with the Congress-led UPA, have come out in public for the 'top job' after the elections. Lalu Prasad Yadav has also stated that he may extend his support to Ram Vilas for the coveted post of prime minister. The regional warhorses have decided to test waters in anticipation of an unpredictable situation, post elections.

These regional leaders are not ordinary political gamblers. If V P Singh and Chandra Shekhar (1989-91) or H D Deve Gowda and

Inder Kumar Gujral (1996-98) could emerge from nowhere and be catapulted from obscurity to fame overnight, Pawar or Paswan or Jayalalithaa or Chandrababu Naidu and never say die H D Deve Gowda can also stake their claim in the event of a fractured electoral verdict. Of course, Amar Singh has added Mulayam Singh to the list of prime ministerial aspirants.

The Communists may have decided to play the role of kingmaker. But the Congress and the BJP are not going to easily surrender their right to nominate their own candidate for the leadership of a coalition government at the Centre after the next Lok Sabha polls.

Lal Krishna Advani has been projected as the leader of a BJP-led coalition government at the Centre and he has got full endorsement from the BJP National Council. The need for such an endorsement in support of Advani's candidature by the BJP's highest policy-making body was felt because Bhairon Singh Shekhawat has sent clear signals to the leadership about his own candidature on the plea that he has 'friends' in all parties and that he would be in a better position to form a BJP-led coalition government. There was also a storm in the tea cup when a section of big business asserted that Narendra Modi would be a very capable and competent person for the post of prime minister. The BJP had to discourage all such challenges to Advani's candidature.

If the BJP has settled its leadership issue, Congress president Sonia Gandhi has clearly come out in favour of Manmohan Singh as prime minister again. She knows that ambitious factional leaders within the Congress can go to any extent to achieve their personal goals even at the cost of the electoral prospects of the party to which they claim to belong.

Ambitious factional leaders keep on playing their games and instead of openly opposing Manmohan, they use every opportunity to propose Rahul Gandhi for the 'top post'. However, Sonia has scotched all speculations by indicating that Rahul has to wait. Further, Jayanthi Natarajan and other spokesmen of the Congress have stated that 'there is no vacancy for the top post'. Sonia has also pointed out that factionalism is the danger: the Congress party was defeated in the recent assembly elections in Madhya Pradesh and Chhattisgarh because of factional divisions within the party.

It deserves to be clearly stated that a prime minister is the chief political executive of the whole parliamentary system of government and only he is expected to articulate authoritatively both domestic and foreign policies of a country. A prime minister is not only the real head of the council of ministers, he is the only official spokesman of government's crucial polices both within Parliament and in his dealings with President.

Not only this. A prime minister is the hyphen that joins and, to use Bagahot's apt phrase, the buckle that binds the disparate coalition government in a complex and diverse federal parliamentary democracy. Prime minister has to provide real leadership on the basis of consensus among the coalition partners and he cannot perform this role unless he has a bigger political and social reach and backing than every other single individual coalition partner.

The coalition experiments of V P Singh, Chandra Shekhar, H D Deve Gowda and Inder Kumar Gujral failed because within their government they were in a 'minority' and outside forces were in majority. The experience of previous 'temporary prime ministers' clearly shows that a prime minister from a narrow-based region or sub-region cannot effectively play the role of the leader of government: the prime minister, even in a fragmented coalition system, should have larger political acceptability than those whose political base is co-terminus with one state or a few districts of a state. The Congress party could provide a stable coalition government from 2004 to 2009 because all its partners recognised the pre-eminent place of this party in the country as compared to their limited political reach.

Further, while the political map of India has changed, the powerful external countries are not interested in dealing with an unstable government led by a prime minister who is burdened by domestic political constraints of shifting alliance partners. Prime minister even in a coalition government represents the whole country and only a leader of a national party can function as an effective prime minister. The small political players should be led by a coalition leader of a national party. Otherwise the government at the Centre would be purely temporary and unstable. *21 February 2009, Economic Times*

Electoral Strategy of the Left

The communist parties have played a crucial role in the processes of formation of multi-group based central governments since the 1990s and a situation arose in 1996 when many political groups, for the first time in the history of liberal parliamentary democracy, knocked at the door of Jyoti Basu, a Communist leader, to agree to occupy the post of the prime minister.

The Communists have never looked back from 1989 when V P Singh became the prime minister on the basis of the 'outside' support of the Communists and up to 2009 when the Congress-led UPA government, irrespective of political divorce in 2008, could survive only because of the support of a solid group of 58 Communist MPs.

The Communists had fought major ideological, political and electoral battles primarily directed against the Congress party's national dominance. Finally, when the BJP-led government emerged on the scene from 1998 to 2004, the Communists had to change their electoral strategy.

Their strategy in 2004 elections was determined by their opposition to the forces of militant and violent Hindutva represented by the BJP. The15th Lok Sabha elections of April-May 2009 are taking place at a time when according to the communist parties, it is not the BJP government of 2004 but the Congress-led UPA government which has to be opposed. So their target is to defeat the Congress and the BJP by forming 'non-BJP-non-Congress' alliances.

Communist parties have made efforts to create an alternative alliance and on March 12, the four Left Front members along with H D Deve Gowda of Karnataka (Janata Dal – Secular), Chandrababu

Naidu of Andhra Pradesh (TDP) and a representative of J Jayalalithaa (AIADMK) assembled in Karnataka to formally announce the alternative policies and programmes of the third front.

Prakash Karat, and Sitaram Yechury along with A B Bardhan of the CPI have stated that 'If India has to be strengthened, an alternative to communalism, an alternative to the economic policies which need to be changed to be pro-people, an alternative which will keep the independence of our foreign policy and our dignity in the international community' has to be created.

Incidentally, the policy differences with the UPA government, had led to the walking out of the Communists in 2008 because the Congress was alleged to be deviating from 'traditional independence of foreign policy'.

In a multi-group multi-polar political electoral system, any party or group can become a critical player only if it has a sizeable number of Lok Sabha members.

The communists themselves have to form alliances in different states to contest Lok Sabha elections with a view to increase their own seats. The Left Front is already in place in West Bengal, Kerala and Tripura but in other states the Communists have to form alliances to win more seats.

If the CPI(M) is a pre-eminent player in West Bengal, Kerala and Tripura, the TDP is an important anti-Congress force in Andhra Pradesh. That is why an alliance of TDP, Telengana Raj Samiti (TRS), CPI(M), CPI and Madiga Reservation Porata Samiti (MRPS) has been formed to fight not only Lok Sabha but also state assembly elections.

Naveen Patnaik of the BJD has broken his alliance of 11 years with the BJP but he has not openly played his cards about an alliance with any other party. The Communists have been wiped out from Bihar and UP because of the unstoppable caravan of caste-based politics, and this is the reason why the CPI-ML (20 seats), CPI (8) and CPI(M) (5) have decided to jointly contest the elections in Bihar.

The limitations of Communist-led alliance have also to be kept in mind because the formidable Hindi belt is still out of the picture. Mayawati of UP will reveal her cards only after the elections. Her decision to join one or the other group of parties will be conditioned by the option likely to be exercised by Mulayam Singh.

The contest in Maharashtra and Gujarat, like other states of North India, is between NDA and UPA and hence there will be no Left-led alliance in these two states. J Jayalalithaa has given some seats to the Communists but she is still vacillating in her approach towards alliance politics.

While the Communists are emphatic in their assertion that political situation in 2009 'is not a repeat of the one obtaining in 2004 when six years of BJP misrule and communalism had to be fought as a central goal', the Lok Sabha elections of 2009 have to be fought 'around pro-people economic policies, defence of secularism and for an independent foreign policy'.

Further, Prakash Karat expects there will be a polarisation of political forces after the polls which would keep both the combinations led by the Congress and the BJP at bay. The third front, according to him, would occupy the 'central stage with crucial role of the left parties'.

But the question is can they really contain Hindutva forces. Is it not premature to write off the aggressive forces of Hindutva? Unfortunately, the communists are fighting ideological-based political elections along with allies who have a record of political opportunism and contempt for any principled politics. *21 March 2009, Economic Times*

Dreaming of PM's Office: Regional leaders can't assume nations roles

The kite-flying by political leaders, especially those belonging to regional parties, in projecting their candidature for the office of the Prime Minister, seems quite amusing as not only the whole exercise is premature but also a reflection of the wishful thinking of regionalists.

Sharad Pawar had walked out of the Sonia Gandhi-led Congress as he felt that in the new set-up he had no chance of becoming the

Prime Minster of India. But floating a new regional outfit, the NCP, by Pawar, along with PS Sangma and a few others, did not help him achieve his goal. He is now dead serious to stake his claim for prime ministership as this Lok Sabha election is his last chance to achieve his life-long ambition of a Maratha becoming the Prime Minster. Being a *Marathi manoos*, he has garnered the Shiv Sena's support.

The Left is trying to mobilise regional parties like the BSP, the JD(S), the Telugu Desam Party, the TRS and the AIADMK to contest the Lok Sabha election from a common platform, maintaining equidistance from the Congress and the BJP. This is not the only political goal of regionalists who have decided to form a front with the Communists. Every regional party is led by an ambitious leader who has expressed the desire to occupy the office of the Prime Minister. Ms Mayawati has claimed a Dalit's right to occupy the coveted post as all Prime Ministers till now have been from 'upper' castes; the time, she says, has come to break this tradition. Not only that, she has asserted her claim on the basis that she is administrating the largest State with a sizeable presence of MPs.

Communists and other regional allies of Ms Mayawati are worried about this development and D Raja of the CPI had to state that 'first bring the numbers, then we will talk about prime ministership'. Ms Jayalalithaa and HD Deve Gowda are also in the race and Jyoti Basu has said that while it is difficult for the 'Third Front' to win the election, the efforts of the Communists and their allies are politically very significant.

The only issue is that the 'Third Front' has a galaxy of leaders who are candidates for prime ministership. Ram Vilas Paswan of the UPA has announced that he is the 'real Dalit leader' with enough experience to occupy the highest office. Regional leaders have created personality-based organisations and are free to make any announcement without referring to any collective decision-making party structures, and this is the reason that Ms Mayawati or Pawar or Paswan can take any decision at their own sweet will.

The national parties like the Congress and the BJP discuss and decide on the issue of party leader after different individuals stake their claims and finally these parties zero in on one name considering the consensus within the party. When there was a rumour in the Congress projecting Rahul Gandhi for the post of Prime Minister, Ms Sonia Gandhi's announcement that Manmohan Singh is thei party's candidate silenced the internal discussion about the alternative contenders for the post. The BJP has declared LK Advani as its candidate for the Prime Minister's job and he has full support of the Sangh Parivar. When a few corporates extended their support to Gujarat Chief Minister Narendra Modi for the coveted post, the BJP leadership, including Modi himself, reiterated that Advani was their candidate.

The contest between Mrs Indira Gandhi and Morarji Desai for the post of prime ministership substantiates the argument that sometimes national parties are involved in the struggle for choosing a candidate for public office. Regionalists have a clear choice because Ms Mayawati or Paswan or Pawar are their own masters and their party is their shop. Should such sectional and sectarian leaders become the Prime Minister?

A Prime Minister should be perceived as an umpire by 30 State Governments of India and the Union Territories. The Union Government is meant for the whole country and there will be protests if the Centre is seen to be aligned towards any one region. Regions in India are mini-lingual, mini-cultural and mini-ethnic entities and these 'multiple mini-Indians' have to be administered as a 'whole' by the Centre under the leadership of a Prime Minister.

Prakash Singh, a retired IPS official, has written in his book that a Prime Minister asked him about non-representation of his caste in the police force and fortunately such a person with limited perspective remained Prime Minister for six months only. Indian unity is threatened by such regional chauvinists and a proper equilibrium between the Centre and region can be maintained only by a Prime Minister who is not dependent on limited local support.

The point is not whether a Prime Minister should have a national and international perspective which is essential for governance of the country. Regional leaders should be Cabinet members who can bring regional problems to the fore, but the Prime Minister should be able to reconcile conflicting regional demands by providing a national perspective in decision-making. The Union Government is the centre of power in the Indian federal arrangement of governance and it cannot be left as hostage to the regionalists who are always engaged in fighting local battles for local benefits. *1 April 2009, Pioneer*

Competitive Political Democracy

Most liberal political theorists are justifiably proud of the success of our grand experiment of electoral political democracy. They point to the relatively high turnout of voters in successive Lok Sabha elections, a figure which has steadily risen from about 45% in 1951-2 to 58.1% in the last elections in 2004. More important, unlike in many western democracies, there is no evidence of either fatigue or voter withdrawl from the electoral process. Clearly, if an active participation of voters in a competitive electoral democracy is any evidence of the success of the democratic experiment, India can legitimately claim to have succeeded in laying down the foundations of a participatory, democratic political system.

Second, by constitutionally mandating 'reservation' of seats for the hitherto marginalized Scheduled Caste and Tribe groups, accounting for as many as 120 out of 543 seats in Parliament, and many more in state assemblies and the third tier of panchayats and municipalities, the Indian political arrangement has successfully modified and made more inclusive the principle of universal adult franchise based on the first-past-the-post system of choosing representatives. Over time, not just socially oppressed groups like Dalits and Tribals, but other marginalized groups like Yadavs, Kurmis, Jats and so on, have come to occupy a central and critical position in our electoral politics and governance. Finally, even erstwhile secessionist groups like the Mizos and Nagas, as also those others like the Naxalites who believed that 'power flows out of the barrel of the gun', have been persuaded to abandon the path of violence and participate in the electoral process.

An upshot of the above narrative is that Indian electoral democracy has successfully accommodated various social groups by providing them with constitutional rights based on 'special reservations' for 'representation' in the crucial centres of decision-making of the institutions of governance. Many historically 'socially excluded' groups today feel more empowered because they have got a share in power as a result of their special representation in the electoral political process. This description, however, captures only one part of the story.

But just what kind of social transformation has taken place because of the functioning of an electoral process based on universal adult franchise? It is routinely claimed that relatively politically apathetic Indians have not only become politically active, but also socially assertive and demanding because of the power of right to vote. The Indian voter is conscious of his power to elect and reject political representatives and parties and, for the first time in Indian history, ordinary Indians have been enabled to punish their political leaders. While true, this does appear to be a rather limited understanding of social change brought about by universal adult franchise in the social consciousness of the voters. Even as ordinary Indians have become more aware about their rights as citizens, the democratic project of fundamentally transforming society cannot be reduced to electoral participation because the social agenda of basic transformation demands an awareness about the fundamental issues facing society and an enhanced capability to liberate themselves from the inherited social categories of the past.

The Indian National Congress which nurtured the infant system of universal adult franchise not only followed mobilization strategies directed towards winning the support of multiple and diverse social groups during the elections, but also advocated programmes and policies for the benefit of different and distinct social groups. This particular and special social group-based political and electoral mobilizational strategy of all 'bourgeois and peasant-based parties' has over time given birth to compartmentalised and segmentary levels of awareness and social consciousness. This is possibly one reason why group-specific demands are raised by representatives of the people and group-specific benefits are distributed by the coalition of social classes and groups when they come to occupy political power.

An instructive example of this fragmented approach to social problems is the enthusiastic pursuit of policies concerning caste and sub-caste-based reservations by every 'member of the ruling bloc', across political parties. If there is any political consensus in India on any one issue among all the strata of the ruling bloc, it is on the policy of reservations of seats in parliamentary, legislative or panchayati raj institutions and for appointments to public institutions without underestimating the importance of the many struggles that different social groups have launched.

Can such a society pursue an all-India agenda of democratic social transformation for social equality? The answer is a big no. India continues to witness struggles around caste-based demands in part because our level of social consciousness has become co-terminus with caste or sub-caste based fragmented identities. Unsurprisingly, therefore, all-India united democratic struggles of the oppressed and exploited 'rural and urban underclasses' have failed to pose an effective challenge to the exploiting ruling bloc because the 'underclasses' are themselves completely fragmented on the basis of their identity-based levels of social existence around caste or sub-caste.

This has also helped the ruling classes and their political and bureaucratic governing classes to manage an exploitative and unequal society. Hence, the central paradox facing both theorists and practitioners of democracy: How do we explain the perpetuation of social inequalities in a democracy which claims, and rightly so, to have provided new opportunities to precisely those social groups who were always kept out of the power structure because of their history of social discrimination. Each one of us, liberal or Marxist, has to confront a basic question regarding who rules over India and how India is governed.

The different schools of liberal theory, irrespective of their inner conflicts and tensions, assert that only elected representatives of the people rule in India on the basis of an institutional system of governance based on checks and balances. Not only do we have a participatory system of democracy, the legitimacy of 'rulers' is based on the consent of the ruled, in part because of efforts to provide quota-based representation to all those social groups which needed special provisions and legal support for finding a berth in the centres of power.

Further, Indian democracy is responsive to multiple and varied interests of diverse groups. The result is a responsible and responsive democratic government which has followed a gradualist reformist social agenda for the amelioration of the living conditions of the needy and really vulnerable groups in society. Unfortunately, this rather simplistic analysis does not help identify the real rulers who actually exercise power in a democracy. Surely, it is not the case that the urban and rural underclasses elect representatives for the perpetuation of their misery or that the struggling poor masses of India exercise their right to vote for strengthening and solidification of capitalism and agrarian class exploitation and oppression?

It is undeniable that the electoral political system of democracy has transformed Indian society as also generated new levels of awareness among the mass of voters. This is a positive consequence of a competitive democratic political system. The negative side is that on the plea of providing new opportunities of representation to the marginal and socially excluded groups in society, the ruling classes have helped entrench a completely fragmented social system such that new levels of awareness and consciousness have become co-terminus with specific and distinct identity groups like caste or sub-caste. Given this social dialectic of Indian democracy, we should not be surprised that the rising levels of awareness have not translated into an all-India agenda of democratic struggles against the forces of oppression and suppression. *April, 2009, Seminar 596*

Struggles for the Political Centre

Political parties and numerous diverse groups are engaged in a cut-throat electoral competition to reach the summit of power with the sole purpose of exercising control over the central government. If the sole purpose of electoral competition among parties is to win elections and form a government at the Centre, attention deserves to be focused on the challenges of governance which the central government is expected to face in 2009.

First, the Congress, the BJP and the communists, on the basis of their own national perspective have themselves identified the basic tasks which have to be performed by a new central government. The major concern of all the three important political formations is the central issue of economic meltdown, which has created an all-round crisis in every sector of the economy. Indian economy is globally integrated and it is just not possible to escape from the serious negative impact of the great crash of 2008.

Second, it is not only the industrial economy or the service sector but also the farm sector that is facing serious crisis, which is dramatised by the suicides committed by the farmers. M S Swaminathan, chairman, National Commission on Farmers, has drawn attention to the plight of 100 million-plus small farmers who are suffering from the problems of credit crisis and food security crisis. Not only this.

There is sluggish demand for jobs outside agriculture and a little comfort has been provided by the National Rural Employment Guarantee scheme, but many more schemes for the improvement of living conditions of small and marginal farmers are urgently needed if the central government is expected to deal effectively with agrarian crisis.

Third, Prime Minister Manmohan Singh had stated on April 5, 2009 that 'Communalism, terrorism and Naxalism' are great challenges facing the government of India. The BJP has promised in its manifesto to pursue 'muscular policies' to fight against terrorism, and on April 7, 2009, a Strategy Paper was issued under the caption

The Congress Party's pledge-Protecting India from Terror' and the CPI(M) in its manifesto has committed itself to 'tackle terror, including Maoist and Hindutva terror'.

Manifestos, election campaigning and policy statements of the Congress, the BJP and the CPI(M) clearly show that all these three parties have shown common concern for challenges and problems facing the whole country. They have focused special attention on 'economic turbulence which has originated from the US and is continuing to rock the country's economy'and all these three parties have shown complete agreement on the threat which India is facing from 'terrorism'.

This is the political scenario in which the Lok Sabha elections of 2009 are taking place and any coalition government at the Centre will have to take very hard decisions on foreign, domestic, economic and security policies. Any soft-pedalling on the foreign and domestic policy front by the government will not only further aggravate economic crisis but also make crisis-ridden divided India vulnerable to external pressures and diktats of foreign governments or hostile terrorist groups.

It is not a question of stability or instability of a coalition system of government at the Centre which can provide meaningful leadership to the whole country. The real question is that an all-India government should have a national rallying point which can bind together varied and disparate casteist, regionalist and sub-regionalist members of the coalition government.

Prakash Karat has asserted that the 'present logic of the situation' is in favour of the emergence of non-Congress, non-BJP, Communist-led third front of secular groups which will be able to provide new directions to foreign and domestic policies of the country.

The issue is: can the left parties, with national perspective, become a rallying point of a government consisting of regional, sub-regional and casteist political formations? The communist parties have a national perspective of governance but their capacity to bring disparate so-called secular groups on a common policy platform is quite limited because the electoral logic is that the communist parties cannot have enough number of Lok Sabha MPs which can make them either pre-eminent or significant first among equals in a coalition government.

Buddhadeb Bhattacharjee has raised the issue national vision while trying to form a new government at the Centre: 'Who is going to run the country. That is the big question in this election. Being regional parties, they can not see beyond the state perspective... We are now engaged in the party to form a new government at the Centre'.

If the communist parties cannot play the role of an effective leadership of a coalition government, the Congress and the BJP remain claimants for leading a coalition at the Centre. Hence, the real contest for leadership of the coalition government at the Centre is between the Congress and the BJP and any one of these parties will make real effort to form a coalition around itself.

Ideological hat of secularism or socialism which is worn by many contenders and pretenders during the elections has become shapeless and faceless because after the elections every small casteist, regionalist and sub-regionalist group will opt for the winning horse without caring for ideology.

The BJP could remain in power at the Centre from 1998 to 2004 and the six years experiment was enough to substantiate the argument that the logic of opportunities provided by becoming a partner of a coalition is superior to the phoney commitment to the value of secularism and anti-Hindutva.

The Congress party, a secular formation, is really confronting the Hindu communal BJP, and it can succeed only if it can secure 150 plus seats in the15th Lok Sabha. Congress and communists are 'natural allies' in a common struggle against the threat posed by the forces of Hindutva.

The coalitional central government cannot have any political capability if it consists of a motley crowd of disparate regionalists whose sole interest is to exercise power at the Centre for local benefits. A national minimum consensus is required to deal with complex global and interrelated foreign policy and crisis of domestic economy. Such a consensus can be implemented only by a coalition which is led by one or the other political formation with the national perspective. 25 *April* 2009, *Economic Times*

Making Sense of Congress Victory

The real story of the Sonia Gandhi-led Congress begins with the Lok Sabha elections of 1998 and 1999 when its electoral performance was the lowest in the long history of post-independence Congress including the post-Emergency elections of 1977. Its active cadre and leadership were also in a defeatist and pessimistic mood.

Further, the Congress of Sonia Gandhi of 1998 was in a shambles because Narasimha Rao-Sitaram Kesri leadership from 1991 to 1997 had completely destroyed the credibility of the party by alienating its Dalit and Muslim social constituencies. Consequently, the party was reduced to a rump and had to face the growing challenge of the aggressive right wing Hindutva forces.

The minority communities also developed the feeling that the Congress party, which could not prevent the demolition of Babri mosque, had ceased to be a secular saviour of the minorities and so they shifted their electoral support to secular regional leaders like Mulayam Singh and Lalu Prasad. It was not without reason that Congress got only 141 Lok Sabha seats in 1998 with 25.82% of votes polled, and in 1999, it obtained only 114 seats with 28.30% of polled votes.

This trend of low performance by the Congress was not reversed even in the Lok Sabha elections of 2004 when it obtained 145 seats with 26.53% of votes. The Congress-led UPA government received popular political endorsement in the Lok Sabha elections of 2009 by securing 206 seats out of 543 and 29% of the votes in its favour. Further, its traditional social constituencies consisting of Dalits along with Muslim and Christian minorities have come together under the social umbrella of the secular Congress party.

What is the explanation for the 're-emergence' of the Congress in

2009? First, the Sonia-led Congress built itself step by step, beginning with 1998. The message of the Lok Sabha elections of 2004 with 145 seats only was rightly interpreted by the leadership to mean that it will have to show real 'performance' if the party has to go further on revival path. In pursuit of this target, the Congress followed very 'cautious' policies of coalition-making and governance with a view to win the continuing support of the various strata of Indian society.

The BJP had targeted the Congress-led UPA government by alleging that the real centre of power was Sonia Gandhi and not Prime Minister Manmohan Singh. Sonia and Manmohan proved that in reality party president and the PM were working in complete harmony with one another. The pubic of India did not get any evidence that the two were working at cross purposes.

Incidentally, open conflict between the PM and party president has been a tradition of post-Independence Congress, beginning with Nehru versus Purushotam Das Tandon and Indira Gandhi versus Nijalingappa or even Kamraj.

Sonia and Manmohan from 2004 to 2009 worked in a manner that differences of opinion between the two, if any, were resolved at their own levels. Even factional leaders of the Congress had no stories to plant in the media to show any clash between the PM and Congress president. Only the BJP and the sangh parivar kept on raising the non-issue of 'dual centres of power'. This image of a harmonious leadership clicked with the voters.

Sonia Gandhi, who was haunted by the Bofors controversy, knew that any allegation of corruption, real or fictitious, against the highest officeholder of the country, would completely delegitimise the leadership. Incidentally, the Congress component of the UPA government from 2004 to 2009 was never targeted by the opposition for indulging in corruption and the image of Prime Minister Manmohan Singh and A K Antony as defence minister strengthened the belief among the common people that Sonia is committed to clean government. Not only this. A great loyalist, Natwar Singh, was shown the door when he was embroiled in the Iraqi food for oil controversy.

The BJP lost the 2004 Lok Sabha elections on the India Shinning slogan, projected on the basis of the NDA government's economic policies of liberalisation, privatisation and globalisation from 1998 to 2004. Manmohan Singh had always been projected as the 'original economic reformer' and founder of the New Economic Policy of liberalisation.

If the BJP could not win an electoral endorsement on the basis of its economic policies, it would have been impossible for the Congress to maintain its support base of 2004 elections by selling the high rate of economic growth as its sterling achievement. The Sonia-led Congress has not only improved upon the performance of 145 seats of 2004 to 206 seats in 2009, it has also won over a large section of the rural and urban underclasses, especially at a time when the global economic recession is haunting the economy.

The 'economist' PM was put on the task of chalking out the programme of economic growth. Further, Sonia Gandhi constituted the National Advisory Council of some public spirited individuals who were working at the grassroot levels of society and involved in ameliorating the living conditions of the poor. Sonia-led NAC suggested that the government should formulate the Right to Information Act with a view to make governance transparent and accountable.

The NAC also suggested that 'economic growth with human face' required a national rural employment guarantee scheme which would provide direct employment to the rural poor for at least 100 days on wages to be paid by the government exchequer. The scheme was launched in February 2006 and the doubting Thomases had ridiculed it as populist subsidy system.

The three years of implementation of NREGA brought relief to 4.5 crore rural households and the central government spent Rs. 40,000 crore on NREGA, out of which Rs. 29,000 crore were paid as wages. Further, agrarian crisis was aggravated by suicides committed by indebted farmers and the UPA government launched a massive 'loan waiver' scheme.

The restoration and revival of the declining Congress solely depended on the performance of Congress-led UPA government and the harmonious working relationship between the PM and the party president. The Congress revival is the direct consequence of traditional left-of-centre image and programmes of the Congress.

Sonia's Congress brought back Nehruvian traditions of secularism and democracy based on left-of-centre programmes. Congress rediscovered its roots in the ideological framework of social justice and secular modernisation of a society and the voters found this Congress acceptable. 3 *May* 2009, *Economic Times*

Paradoxes Facing Communists

Marx, Lenin and Mao had repeatedly emphasised that believers and practitioners of communist ideology have to concretely identify 'primary' and 'secondary', 'antagonistic' and 'non-antagonistic' social contradictions and evolve political strategies to counter and fight against 'primary political opponents'. The CPI(M) has concretely identified that sovereignty of the Indian state is threatened by US imperialism and secular nationalism is under a sustained political and ideological attack from the forces of Hindu fundamentalism represented by the sangh parivar and its political outfit the BJP.

Prime Minister Manmohan Singh has repeatedly maintained that India-US nuclear deal is for 'access to nuclear technology and fuel' and has asserted that such nuclear agreement in no way would impact our 'independent foreign policy'. The communists, on the contrary, have firmly believed that foreign policy based on strategic alliance with the US has made India a camp follower of imperialism. There is absolutely no meeting ground between the Congress and the communists on their approach towards India-US relationship.

The communists have launched an all-out offensive to delegitimise and defeat the Congress with a view to 'liberate India' from the stanglehold of US imperialism. The Left on the basis of their own political and parliamentary strength cannot launch a successful political offensive against the Congress party, and they have decided to seek support from every other political formation like the BJP the other 'enemy' of the communists'.

Not only this. They have mobilised even those political formations in their favour which had played a significant role in not only legitmising Hindu fundamentalism but had also kept them in power at the Centre from 1998 to 2004.

Chandrababu Naidu of the TDP, a new ally of the communists, was a key actor in keeping the Vajpayee government in power at the Centre. And Mayawati, another of their new-found ally, had actively campaigned in favour of Narendra Modi-led BJP in Gujarat assembly elections of 2002, which had been held after the post-Godhra genocide.

The communists would have to do a lot of explaining to the Indian secular and democratic social, political and intellectual groups about their 'decision' to defeat the UPA government at all costs, including direct and indirect support by the Hindu fundamentalists and their fellow travellers like Naidu, Mayawati, Badal, Chautala, et al. Marx

, Lenin and Mao had asked communists of every country to choose their allies with great care. During World War II, G Dimitrov, a noted Marxist intellectual, had suggested the formation of an Anti-Fascist United Front to 'defeat fascist forces'. Indian communists cannot defeat the Indian variant of fascism represented by the sangh parivar, on their own, and they have to make every effort to strengthen a United Front of secularists including the Congress.

Marxists have always characterised the Congress 'as a weak secular bourgeois party' and there is no reason to change this description about the social base of the Congress. It is disingenuous on the part of the communists to justify their strategy of taking support from Hindu fundamentalists and casteists on the ground that the Congress had done the same thing while defeating V.P. Singh (1990) H.D. Deve Gowda (1997) and I.K. Gujral (1998). Further, the argument advanced by the communists that 'if the BJP wants to vote against (UPA), they have a right to do so' is a specious one.

It is not just a question of voting in the Lok Sabha: the ideological position taken by the communists has serious consequences for the future of the Secular Democratic Republic of India. Any direct or indirect help to the forces of Hindu fundamentalism will definitely weaken further the secular forces. Already the BJP (and every other member of the sangh parivar) has gained in strength and extended its area of influence from J&K to Karnataka, from Punjab to Orissa. Today, major states like Rajasthan, MP, Maharasthra, Gujarat and UP are witnessing the forward march of Hindutva. Further, the sangh parivar has extended and strengthened its ideological and institutional network in the tribal belt of Rajasthan to MP, to Orissa and Chhattisgarh.

Further, every state government run by the BJP has actively facilitated the penetration of ideology of Hindu Rashtra, much to the dismay of Muslims, Christians and other minorities. As late as July 12, 2008, in an interview to a national daily, L K Advani had stated that 'Hindutva should be equated to Bharatiyata. Indianness and Hindutva are synonymous. Don't make a distinction between the two. It should mean nationalism essentially'. Advani is a carrier of the most dangerous ideology and world view, which goes fundamentally against the spirit of the 'idea of India' enshrined in the secular republican Constitution of the country.

Indian communists claim to be ideologically opposed to the idea of 'Hindu India' and the sangh parivar, which is the torch bearer of this dangerous ideology. To paraphrase Eric Hobsbawm, a Marxist historian, the spectre of Hindu fundamentalism haunts India and, to hark back Dimitrov, there is a need to form a United Front against Hindu communalists and fascists. This is the real challenge before the Indian communists. It also deserves to be mentioned here that secular forces in India today are not confronted with a weakling like the Jana Sangh of the Nehru era because, the sangh parivar is spatially entrenched in states and regions where communists do not have any presence.

Further, while Congress has vacated its earlier dominant all-India presence, the BJP is moving forward and confronting politically and ideologically the secular forces. Narendra Modi was not dismissed even after genocide of post-Godhra because the BJP-led NDA government was in power at the Centre in 2002.

The communist parties claim to be fighting US imperialism and communalism but in the process, consciously and unconsciously, they are weakening the secular parties and formations. Marx had warned that human beings should also be worried about the 'unintended consequences of their actions'. In the current situation, though the communists have every right to use every fora including the Lok Sabha to oppose a strategic alliance with an imperialist America, supporting the right wing communal forces, directly or indirectly, with a view to weaken secular forces will be disastrous for the future development of democratic India.

Can Left and Congress Align Again? To defeat hindutva, they must join together

Political interventions and decisions by political parties are always dictated and decided by the logic of concrete situations created by social dialectics of a concrete society. Indian social dialectics-at-work has created a situation where every political and social formation has to search for allies and make alliances to form a government at the Centre. The Communist parties have an antagonistic contradiction with the Hindu Rashtravadis represented by the Sangh.

The Congress party, like the communists, is committed to oppose the ideology of religion-based politics of the Sangh. The Congress and the communists recognised the need to fight against Hindutva by joining hands after the Lok Sabha elections of 2004. The communists withdrew support to the Congress and have decided to form an anti-Congress and anti-BJP alternative political platform for the forthcoming Lok Sabha elections.

It deserves to be clearly stated that only the Congress and communists can together confront the threat posed by the politics of Sangh Parivar because the alternative alliance partners of the communists are well-known political weather cocks and opportunists. Many examples can be provided to substantiate the argument that the anti-Congress and anti-BJP alternative alliance politics cannot be a viable proposition because all regionalist parties are slippery political characters and none of them considers the BJP as number one enemy of the secular fabric of India.

The Congress and communists therefore have to work together with a 'minimalist' anti-BJP and a few pro-poor welfare policies common programme. Congress is the largest single secular political and social formation and the Left is also a pillar of anti-communal secular politics. Congress and the Left will eventually work together because none of the two on its own can fight against Hindutva. The logic of social dialectics is that these two secular social forces should join hands to oppose Hindutva. Congress and the communists have no option but to come together to fight the Hindutva forces because, finally, both need one another due to their common secular belief system.

Lok Sabha Elections: 2009

The Verdict of May 16, 2009 has changed the political landscape because the Congress party and its pre-election allies like the DMK of Tamil Nadu, National Conference of Jammu and Kashmir, the National it Congress Party of Maharashtra and the Trinamool Congress of West Bengal have received a clear mandate to form the Congress-led government at the Centre. The major political opponents of the Congress-alliance like the BJP-led alliance and the Communist parties-formed front were electorally reduced to a minority status vis-à-vis the majority status attained by the Congress alliance. The focus of analysis of Lok Sabha electoral picture should not remain confined only on the major political players because Indian democracy is plagued with the problematic of not only proliferation of parties but thousands of so-called 'unattached-Independent' candidates also participate in the lections. The Lok Sabha elections of 2009 witnessed the involvement of 369 parties out of which only 37 parties have won some seats in the Lok Sabha consisting of 543 members. A total of 332 out of 369 parties failed to send even a single member to the Lok Sabha. Further, during the 2004 Lok Sabha elections, 215 parties including six national parties and 36 state parties participated in the electoral contest. This proliferation of parties and Independent candidates creates difficult management and law and order problems for the Election Commission of India and this is the reason that elections are conducted in a staggered manner with a view to ensure free, fair and fearless holding of elections.

A few salient features of Indian electoral participatory democracy may be mentioned to understand the context of the Congress party victory in the Lok Sabha elections of 2009.

First: Indian voter has never shown any sign of fatigue

Table I: The Pattern of Voting

Lok Sabha Elections		*Major Assembly Elections**		
Year	*Turnout (%)*	*Year*	*No. of States*	*Turnout (%)*
1952	45.7	1952	22	46
1957	47.7	1957	13	48
1962	55.4	1960-62	15	58
1967	61.3	1967	20	61
1971	55.3	1971-72	21	60
1977	60.4	1977-78	24	59
1980	57.2	1979-80	16	54
1985	63.1	1984-85	18	58
1989	61.9	1989-90	18	60
1991	55.9	1993-96	25	67
1996	57.9	19990-03	30	65
1998	62.1	2004-08	30	70
1999	59.9			
2004	58.1			
2009	58.0			

* A 'major' round of assembly elections is defined here as one which involved elections to at least 2000 assembly constituencies. The figures given for the first three general elections here are lower than reported in many other places. The figures here adjust for the double and triple member constituencies in those elections where the number of votes used to be higher than the number of voters.

The above Table Clearly reveals that voters' participation beginning from 1952 to 2009 except 1952 and 1957, has been much more than 50 percent to 60 percent and the early apathy shown by the voters in the Lok Sabha elections of 1952 and 1957 has come to an end.

Second, Democratic Theory of representation to 'include' socially disadvantaged groups has not only been accepted by the Constitution of India, the all-India national parties and state level parties have actively implemented the policy of 'Reservations of seats for Scheduled Castes and Scheduled Tribes' in Elections. Further, a purely Dalit based party like the Bahujan Samaj Party has contested elections both for the Lok Sabha and State Assemblies by mobilizing Dalit voters.

The above Table clearly shows a few interrelated developments in the electoral history of India like the increasing number of candidates who are involved in electoral battles, and the increasing role of regional or state level parties in electoral competition. The national or all-India parties are faced with a challenge from state-level parties and electoral spaces are occupied by both the All-India and the state level parties which reveal the federal diversity of Indian electoral democracy. This is an important trend in Indian political

Another Table III helps us to understand the shifting nature of places or rankings of national and state level parties from first Lok Sabha elections to the Fourteenth Lok Sabha.

The Table III confirms the placement, replacement and displacement of once dominant Congress party, the gradual emergence of Jan Sangh/Bhartiya Janata Party, closely followed by the CPI-CPM on the electoral map. The Lok Sabha elections gradually brought down both Congress and BJP and the Communists achieved their peak along with electoral successes of many multiple region and sub-regional parties and groups.

A political miracle happened in 2009 when Congress crossed and obtained 206 out of 543 Lok Sabha seats (Table IV).

The above Table IV clearly shows that while Congress gained electorally in the Lok Sabha elections of 2009, the BJP and the Left parties lost very heavily in electoral battle. The regional parties maintained their heavy presence like previous elections.

Table II: Social Inclusive Electoral Democracy and Number of Parties

Parameters	*1951*	*1957*	*1962*	*1967*	*1971*	*1977*	*1980*	*1984-85*	*1989+*	*1991*	*1996*	*1998*	*1999*	*2004*
Seats	489	494	494	520	518	542	542	541	529	537	543	543	543	543
Reserved	98	107	109	114	112	116	120	119	117	120	120	120	120	120
Candidates	1894	1519	1985	2369	2784	2439	4629	5492	6160	8749	13952	4750	4648	5435
National Parties	14	4	6	7	8	5	6	7	8	9	8	7	7	6
Number	76	73.1	78.5	76.1	77.8	84.7	85.1	77.9	79.3	80.6	69.1	68.0	67.1	62.9
State Parties														
Number	39	11	11	14	17	15	19	19	20	28	30	30	40	36
Vote Shares (%)	8.1	7.6	9.3	9.7	10.2	8.8	7.7	12.0	9.3	13.1	22.4	18.8	26.9	28.9%
Eligible Voters (In cores)	17.3	19.4	21.6	24.9	27.4	32.2	35.6	40.0	49.9	51.2	59.3	60.6	61.9	67.2
Poll Percentages	44.9	45.4	655.4	61.0	55.3	60.5	56.9	64.0	562.0	55.9	57.9	62.0	60.0	58.1
Polling Stations	NA	NA	238031	243693	342918	373910	436813	506058	580798	591020	767462	772681	774651	687473
Spending by Election Commission (in Rs. Crore)	10.5	5.9	7.3	10.8	11.6	23.0	54.8	81.5	154. 2	359.1	597.3	666.2	880.0	1300.0

Source: Election Commission, Text: HT Research.

In summation, it may be stated that if minimalist definition of democracy is accepted, India has successfully conducted fifteen Lok Sabha elections on the basis of more than one party. Political parties have competed for people's vote and governments have been formed on the basis of vote of the people. If maximalist definition of democracy is accepted, contestation and participation, as pillars of competitive democracy in a free society, are quite visible and observable. Indian electoral democracy is on the march.

The Indian Security State: Agendas of concern

The indecent haste shown by Political Executive and Parliament on December 16-17, 2008 while dealing with security related issues substantiates the argument that security and defence agenda of the Indian state has become pre-eminent and the social agenda of democracy has been reduced to a secondary and non-essential status.

The terrorist attack of September 11, 2001 on the New York World Trade Centre has become a defining moment in the contemporary history of American society because the dominant public discourse not only among the pubic policy makers but also in the multiple centres of American public and intellectual life has been conditioned solely by the goal of 'War on Terror'. President George Bush, the Chief Political Executive, fully supported by every strata of the American ruling classes waged aggressive military operations against sovereign states and curbed domestic freedoms of American citizens on the basis of a plea that 'America and civilized world has to be saved from global terrorism'. It is absolutely wrong to suggest that only George Bush is responsible for the barbaric treatment of Iraqi detainess at Abu Ghabrib and it deserves to be unambiguously stated that every American is accountable for the indefinite detention at Guantanamo Bay.

David Miliband a Minister of Britain, whose government had fully supported American aggressive politics stated on January 16, 2009 that '...we must uphold our commitments to human rights and civil liberties both at home and abroad. That is surely the lesson

Table III: Shifts in Party Positions

Race Gets Closer	*In 1951, No. 1Was the runaway winner. But over the years, the no. 2 lost by a small margin. In 2009, the old trend of big-margin win made a come back*					
Election Year	1st	2nd	3rd	4th	5th	*Seats*
1951	INC-364	CPI-16	SP-12	KMPP-9	PDF-7	489
1957	INC-371	CPI-27	PSP-19	SCF-6	JHP-6	494
1962	INC-361	CPI-29	SWA-18	JS-14	PSP-12	494
1967	INC-283	SWA-44	BJS-35	DMK-25	CPI/SSP-23	520
1971	INC-352	CPM-25	CPI-23	DMK-23	BJS-22	518
1977	BLD-295	INC-154	CPM-22	ADK-18	SAD-9	542
1980	INC-353	JNP(S)-41	CPM-37	JNP-31	DMK-16	529
1984	INC-414	TDP-30	CPM-22	ADK-12	JNP-10	541
1989	INC-197	JD-143	BJP-85	CPM-33	CPI-12	529
1991	INC-244	BJP-120	JD-59	CPM-35	CPI-14	534
1996	BJP-161	INC-140	JD-46	CPM-32	TMC(M)-20	543
1998	BJP-182	INC-141	CPM-32	SP-20	ADMK-18	543
1999	BJP-182	INC-114	CPM-33	TD-29	SP-26	543
2004	INC-145	BJP-138	CPM-43	SP-36	RKD-24	543

1951: SP-Socialist Party, KMPP- Kishan Mazdoor Praja Party, PDF-Peoples Democratic Front
1957: PSP-Praja Socialist Party, SCF-All India Scheduled Caste Federation, JHP-Jharkhand Party
1962: SWA Swatantra, JS-Jan Sangh 1967: SSP-Samyukta Socialist
1971: BJS-Bharatiya Jan Sangh
1977: BLD Bharatiya Lok Dal, ADK-All India Anna Dravida Munnetra Kazhagam
1980: JNP(S)- Janata Party (Secular)
1996: TMC(M)-Tamil Mannila Congress (Moopanar)

Table IV: Lok Sabha 2009

UPA	263
Congress	206
Trinamul	19
DMK	18
NCP	9
NKNC	3
JMM	2
Rest	6
NDA	159
BJP	116
JD(U)	20
SHS	11
RLD	5
SAD	4
TRS	2
AGP	1
Left	24
CPM	16
CPI	4
RSP	2
AIFB	2
Others	97
SP	23
BSP	21
BJD	14
AIADMK	9
TDP	6
RJD	4
JS(S)	3
Independents	9
Rest	8

Source: KBK Poll graphics

of Guantanamo'. Miliband has made another very important statement on January 16: '...the British security, intelligence, and police services have, since September 2001, been granted vastly expanded powers under highly repressive legislation, which was purportedly created to counter the threat of terrorism'. The western democratic states have enacted many repressive laws in the first decade of the 21st century because every terrorist attack has added to the sense of 'fear and anxiety of citizens' and such an opportunity has been used by the states to increase their own 'coercive powers' with a view to contain the menace of terrorism.

Any excessive concentration of coercive powers in the hand of the functionaries of the state can create serious difficulties for an ordinary law abiding citizen and he may end up as a victim of the misuse and abuse of powers by the executive authority of the state. Indians need not be reminded of a fact that a large number of innocent citizens have suffered loss of freedoms at the hands of functionaries of the state during the actual process of implementation of coercive laws which had been enacted by democratically elected Parliament. India began its democratic journey after Independence on August 15, 1947 and new democracy's first attack on the principle of Rule of Law and Fundamental Rights came in the form of Nehru government's Preventive Detention Act and Indians had not looked back and from the Emergency Regime of Indira Gandhi 1975 to 77 to prevention of Terrorist Act (POTA), the Armed Forces Special Powers Act, the National Act et al.

The Indian state already has on the statute book laws which deal with 'Detention without Trial', but another step has been taken to add to the 'coercive powers of the Indian State' with an argument that terrorist attacks on Mumbai on November 26, 2008 have created a new situation which needs to be responded by powerful anti-Terrorist Law by amending Unlawful Activities (Prevention) Act and the creation of a new National Investigating Agency for the whole country. If September 11, 2001 had become a 'defining moment' for the United Sates, Mumbai events of November 26, 2008 are also considered 'new challenges' to the security of India by the Indian ruling classes and Political Executive of the state. Prime Minister Manmohan Singh on December 13, 2008 while speaking on 'Terrorism, Rule of Law and Human Rights' stated that the government may take some steps which may 'derogate from certain human rights principles' and he further continued 'states are both entitled and obliged to take certain steps that might derogate from human rights principles but only to the extent necessary to meet the security threat'. American or British and now the Indians are sailing in the same boat and responding in a similar manner to the 'anxieties, fears and insecurities' of citizens by providing new legal powers to its coercive instruments so that 'terrorist' threat can be faced effectively and life and liberty of citizens can be defended from attacks of the terrorists.

Curbing Freedoms

Every democratic state, including India, is curbing democratic freedoms of its own citizens in the name of defence of citizens from mindless violet terrorist groups. The State needs more powers than it already has to fight against terrorist attacks and new laws are required to hand over more powers to the coercive apparatuses of the state so that they can effectively deal with the 'New Enemy' of the 21st century. It also deserves to be stated that every state government in India has its own laws for 'detention' of a suspected accused and to fight against insurgency and terrorism, the Assam State government has introduced in the state assembly on January 7, 2009 the Assam Preventive Detention (Amendment) bill 2009 to amend the Assam Preventive Detention Act of 1980 with a new proviso to extend the 'period of preventive detention to 2 years'. Maharashtra Control of Organized Crime (MCOCA) and Maharashtra Anti-Terrorism Squad was already in operation even before November 26, Mumbai attacks.

A few special developments of post-26 November Mumbai terrorist attack deserve to be mentioned to substantiate the argument that like the Post September 11 America, the Indian State is also marching forward with the goal to deal with terrorism on the basis of extraordinary powers and authority. First, the Indian state permitted international investigating and intelligence agencies from the United States, United Kingdom, Israel et al to actively participate and cooperate with Indians in the investigation of terrorist attacks on Mumbai on November 26. The Federal Bureau of Investigation (USA), the Scotland Yard of UK et al and Indian Agencies collectively operated and the USFBI completed its work and John MC Connell, director of US National Intelligence, met the USFBI team in India on December 24, 2008 for a full review of evidence of the terrorist activities in Mumbai. The Government of India was also working in collaboration with the most notorious Central Intelligence Agency (CIA) of the US and even elementary precaution was not taken because the US, British, French, German and Israeli agencies and their governments could use this opportunity and penetrate in the inside corridors of Indian security and intelligence Agencies. Is it the real meaning of India-US Strategic Partnership? Second, Prime Minister Manmohan Singh observed on December 12,2008 '...the Mumbai attacks had created a new consensus to strengthen India's security setup' and '(he) called upon the security establishment to turn the challenge into an opportunity to streamline the systems involving intelligence collection and investigation'.

The Prime Minister on December 12 was not just speaking on the need for efficient working of intelligence and investigating agencies of India, on December 15, the cabinet decided to '(a) Set up a National Investigating Agency (Perhaps on the patterns of US Federal Bureau of Investigation); b) to extend the role of Central Industrial Security Force and agument CISF's strength with 40,000 more personnel and c) provide for longer period in detention without bail for terror accused by amending the Unlawful Activities (Prevention) Act. The government and parliament showed great haste and with the debate lasting only two days both in the Lok Sabha and Rajya Sabha on December 16 and 17 2008, the new laws for the creation of NIA and amendment of UP A 2008 were approved. The government proclaimed that Parliament approved these new laws to deal with 'terrorist related activities' on the basis of a national consensus with a minor difference of opinion expressed by the Communists. The UPA government and political parties represented in Parliament put a seal of approval on anti-terrorist laws only in two days and the ruling classes and all political formations could push New Anti-terrorist Laws because an atmosphere of 'fear and insecurity' prevails in the country especially after November 26 Mumbai attacks.

How could communist parties of India permit the government and Parliament to push such a Law in just two days? At least AR Antualy, a minister in the Manmohan Singh government, observed on December 16, 2008 'I cannot rule out the possibility of this law being misused. This very law which is in the national interest should be made applicable to communal riots'. It is a well known fact that the managers of the State always exploit the vulnerabilities and anxieties of the ordinary citizens and push undemocratic laws on the plea that national security is under threat. The ruling classes and their political representatives have always succeeded in silencing dissenting voices in an atmosphere of national anxieties and the American state after September 11, 2001 and the Indian State after November 26 2008 has succeed in making public opinion quite 'passive' by playing on the idea of country's security is in danger and an 'enemy' is threatening country's integrity. Third, the government has created regional hubs of army trained commandos of the National Security Guard at Mumbai, Chennai, Hyderabad, and Kolkatta.

The story does not end here. The Central government on January 13, 2009 came out with another bright idea of providing an 'exclusive' army trained commandos' 'cover to IT city Bangalore' and '...that Bangalore can be covered by Army's Parachute Regime, which has is training centre in the city'. Further, the government issued an ordinance on January 12, 2009 i.e. Central Industrial Security Force (amendment) 2009 for extending security to 'private and joint sector enterprises' including Hotels like Taj or Oberoi. The upshot of this description is that post-26 November India has changed not for the better, because externally it has bartered away its sovereignty to the US CIA, FBI and internally, the state has moved forward not in the direction of deepening of democracy or rule of law, but in the militarisation and politicisation of the Indian society. The Indian State already has very strong professional Army and paramilitary forces like the Central Reserve Police Force, the Border Security Force along with extremely powerful legal authority structure to deal with problems of 'social disorder' and it has further strengthened its coercive institutions and apparatuses after November 26, on the basis of a rationale that Indian national security is threatened by country's enemies.

Militarisation and Overpoliticisation

The purpose of the above narrative is not only to highlight the undemocratic consequences of the new anti-terrorist Laws approved by Parliament on December 16-17, 2008 but to bring into sharp focus the problems of over militarization and over-policisation of society during the last sixty years of post-Independence India. The Indian state has always responded to every challenge to its authority, whether social or economic or political, by increasing its coercive authority apparatus. The poorest regions of India of Bihar, Madhya Pradesh, Jharkhand, Orissa, Chhattisgarh and Andhra are experiencing struggles of the poorest of the poor tribal and the Scheduled Castes, and the model of response to the movements of the Wretched of the Earth is 'the Greyhounds model of Andhra Pradesh' or poor versus poor model of Salwa Judum of Chhattisgarh. If the working classes take recourse to 'strike' for improvement in their living conditions, the Indian state responds by imposing provisions of the Essential Services Maintenance Act.

The chief ministers were agitated because the newly created National Investigating Agency was considered by them as violation of the Federal arrangements of division of powers provided in the Constitution but they have to be reminded that in their own sates anti-democratic laws exist which have been framed by State Assemblies to deal with people's challenge to the authority of the state governments. Every state government maintains a well-equipped police force including armed constabulary and other para-military organisations with a view to face democratic challenges from various strata of society including the so-called Naxalities. The

Annual Report of the Ministry of Defence of the Government of India for 2007-2008 mentions with pride, 'Apart from the main responsibilities of defending the borders of the country, the armed forces render timely assistance to civil authorities for the maintenance of law and order, essential services and in rescue and relief operations during natural calamities'.

It should be clearly understood that Indian security apparatuses are fully integrated and neither federal division of powers nor external and domestic factors come in the way of the Indian state from deploying every armed or quasi-armed police agencies for curbing any challenge against the authority of the state in any part of the country. India has developed a formal and informal unified system of control for dealing with any security challenge form any part of the country and centralized authority of the Indian state operates in the name of defence of security of the country. Whether Sardar Patel or P. Chidambaram, home ministers have always looked at Indian security from the top to the grassroots and this special feature of highly centralised Indian state in the area of defence and security has been again highlighted during the post-November 26, events of Mumbai. The Indian state has been fighting against the 'enemies' for the last sixty years and every war of India against 'enemies internal or external, Naxals or terrorists has incrementally added to the existing formidable armed capabilities of the state. This is the essence of 'The Security State of India'.

The creation of National Investigation Agency, the 2008 Amendment of Unlawful Activities (Prevention) Act, or Proclamation of Ordinance of 2009 for extending the role of Central Industrial Security Forces or the idea of 'exclusive' military like protection of the IT city of Bangalore should be seen only in this broad context of the growing role of 'coercive' powers of the state in the name of Defence of India. The reality of social dialectics is that if on the one hand, the Indian state has succeeded in confronting every challenge by the armed groups to its authority, on the other, socially progressive democratic forces have also continued to use every democratic space for launching struggles for the deepening of Indian democracy. The Indian state is hypersensitive about the issues of 'national security' but the struggling masses have many a time also succeeded in forcing the state to perform its obligations for the uplift of the living conditions of the poorest of the poor rural and urban underclasses.

Democratic political and social formations should be extremely worried because the Indian Parliament, which has never approved any law or action of the political executive in just two days concerning the livelihood of the oppressed and the exploited strata of society. The post-Mumbai 26 November public atmospherics had made it possible that the political executive could push its agenda about 'security and defence' of India against armed groups but every security and defence oriented legislation has a long term impact on democratic society which will continue even after November 26. The indecent haste shown by Political Executive and Parliament on December 16-17, 2008 while dealing with security related issues substantiates the argument that security and defence agenda of the Indian state has become pre-eminent and the social agenda of democracy has been reduced to a secondary and non-essential status.

Index